LOUD & CLEAR

IN AN ELECTION YEAR

AMPLIFYING THE VOICES OF COMMUNITY ADVOCATES

Edited by Holly Minch
with Kim Haddow and Laura Saponara

ABOUT THE EDITORS

Holly Minch

Holly is the Director of the SPIN Project, a nonprofit group of communications specialists who provide capacity-building to nonprofit public-interest organizations across the nation. SPIN helps organizations increase their effectiveness in influencing debate, shaping public opinion and garnering positive media attention. Prior to joining the SPIN Project, Holly managed media relations for the Sierra Club and designed training programs for the California Science Center and the Center for Environmental Citizenship. Holly also serves in a leadership role with the Young Nonprofit Professionals Network, an organization founded to engage and support future nonprofit and community leaders through professional development, networking and social opportunities for young people involved in the nonprofit community.

Kim Haddow

Kim is the President of Haddow Communications, Inc., a strategic planning, communications consulting and advertising firm founded in 1995 that specializes in branding, targeting, and promoting the work of nonprofit organizations. Present clients include the national Sierra Club, the Apollo Project, Ocean Champions, the Center for SeaChange, and the Pew Center on Global Climate Change. Before starting her own business, Kim worked for eight years at Greer, Margolis, Mitchell, Burns, a political consulting firm where she worked on 22 statewide candidate and initiative campaigns, ranging from the Virginia gubernatorial campaign of Douglas Wilder to codification of *Roe v. Wade* in Washington state.

Laura Saponara

Laura works as a communications consultant to nonprofit organizations, labor unions and foundations. Her clients include social justice and media organizations such as Women's Educational Media, the San Francisco Jewish Film Festival, the SPIN Project, and the Media, Arts and Culture unit of the Ford Foundation. Formerly a communications director with the American Federation of State, County and Municipal Employees (AFSCME), Laura produced materials and training curricula to fortify labor organizing campaigns in the U.S. and Puerto Rico. A board member of Media Alliance in San Francisco, Laura is active in a community-led initiative to elevate consumer rights, community media, and First Amendment considerations during negotiations over the new franchise agreement between the city and the cable company, Comcast Corporation.

TABLE OF CONTENTS

Acknowledgments   vi

Introduction: Your Voice and Your Vote   vii

What is the SPIN Project?   ix

Navigating This Book   x

SECTION I: THE POLITICAL MOMENT

Election-Year Opportunities   3

Building Grassroots Power   9

    Case Study: Turning Out Your Base   12

    Case Study: Mobilize the Immigrant Vote   17

SECTION II: KNOW THE LAW, DON'T FEAR IT

Power, Tax-Free   23

    Checklist: Permissible Election Activities   28

    Checklist: Election Activities of Individuals with 501(c)(3)s   29

Tax-Exempt Organizations and Campaign Activities   30

And Now, a Word from Our Lawyers   33

"I think there is some general confusion. What can we do as a 501(c)(3)? How much e-mail? How much staff time? There are gray areas. When it comes to the more detailed questions, even seasoned organizers don't have the answers."

—Monica Regan, Northern California Citizenship Project

"It's good to be cautious. The reality is—we have political enemies."

—Bianca Encinias, Southwest Network for Environmental and Economic Justice

SECTION III: FRAMING A PROGRESSIVE AGENDA

Framing a Progressive Agenda: The Basics	39
How and Why to Frame	45
Case Study: Frame and Be Heard	49
Case Study: Election-Year Opportunities for Reframing	51
Winning the Battle of the Story	53
Reframing the National Dialogue: Learning from the Right	56

SECTION IV: MOVING YOUR MESSAGE IN THE ELECTIONS CYCLE

Election Cycle Benchmarks	63
Scorecards, Rankings, and Report Cards	68
Highlighting Your Issue with Research and Reports	73
Case Study: The Apollo Alliance Soars	76
We've Gotta Have It: Polls and the Election-Year News Window	78
Opinion Editorials	82
Letters to the Editor	84
Staging Media Events: Grab Attention for Your Issue	87
Case Study: Lemonade Stand	92
Candidate Forums	93
Rapid Response to Conventions	96
Bird Dogs on the Campaign Trail: Holding Candidates Accountable	100
Case Study: Money Watch 2000	104

"Voter registration-tabling, door-to-door...candidate questionnaires for state, local, and federal offices...candidate forums, meetings with candidates, home visits, face time—it's important to educate members about how to do voter registration."

—Maureen O'Connell, Save Our Cumberland Mountains

"Any organization that's mobilizing communities is always going to be under attack. [That's why] we make sure that all staff...understand the rules....We're very vigilant about protecting our nonprofit status."

—Lydia Camarillo, Southwest Voter Registration Project

SECTION V: EMERGING STRATEGIES

Using Internet Tools to Expand Your Audience, Capacity, and Leverage	107
Case Study: MoveOn.org	113
Serious Irreverence: *The Daily Show*	115
The 2004 Independent Media Landscape	117
Are Ballot Initiatives Part of Your Political Toolkit?	121
Case Study: Florida Ballot Initiative	124
Local Networking for National Movement Building: Immigrant Workers' Freedom Ride	127

SECTION VI: CRITICAL CONSTITUENCIES

Battleground Democracy	135
Giving A Latino Voice to the Vote	138
Black Voters Mobilizing for the 2004 Election	141
Know Your Voting Rights	143
Queer Eye for the Straight Voter	145
Engaging Young Voters, 2004 and Beyond	148
Church and Statesmanship	151
Case Study: How Religious Leaders Helped Counter Opposition to a Living Wage	154
Ethnic and Community Media—Use It or Lose It	155
Straight from the Source: Where Philanthropy and Policy Meet	159

SECTION VII: RESOURCES

Political Jargon	167
Resource Lists	168

"Where's the really powerful messaging? That's a real need."

—Maria Rogers Pascual, Northern California Citizenship Project

"If not now, when are you going to step up?"

—Lorna Vogt, Utah Progressive Network

ACKNOWLEDGMENTS

Like a good meal, this book is better for all the spices and flavors that were added to it, and I want to thank all the cooks in the kitchen:

To the Panta Rhea Foundation and the McKay Foundation, I offer my deep gratitude for your investment in this idea, and your investment in the organizations this book is designed to support. It takes more than a few pennies from heaven to fuel the struggle for true democracy—thank you for helping to keep us going.

To each of the contributors, thank you for lending your experiences and ideas to this book. You are the grassroots force for change in America, and I am grateful for all you do to make our country better for all who live here.

To my fellow editors/project managers/word mavens Kim Haddow and Laura Saponara, kudos and gracias. This was a project characterized by big ideas, many variables, and a blink-and-you'll-miss-it timeline. You fearlessly tackled a significant project with gusto and grace.

To copyeditor Nancy Adess, thanks for making us all sound so wise with your thoughtful editing and swift pen. To our lawyers at Silk, Adler and Calvin thanks for keeping us on the right side of the FEC and the IRS.

To the Design Action Collective, much gratitude for your quick work and keen sense of style.

To the staff of the SPIN Project—Robert Bray, Diana Ip, Rosi Reyes, and Heath Wickline—I am grateful for your feedback, good ideas, moral support and, most of all, your patience during the creation of this book. Collaborating with such a fine team makes me grateful to come to work every day.

To all of my Independent Media Institute colleagues, each of whom touched this book in one way or another, I offer humble thanks for all you do. Great big thanks to Max Toth, who researched and compiled the resource section of this book. Special gratitude to Don Hazen, who convinced me this book was possible, and to Octavia Morgan, who convinced me it was doable.

Finally, love and speechless gratitude to my aunt Wendy Byrnes, who continually teaches me by example that just the right combination of vigorous rabble-rousing and quiet coaxing can awaken hearts and change minds.

—Holly Minch

YOUR VOICE AND YOUR VOTE

By Holly Minch

Decision 2000

> *"I have come to the conclusion that politics are too serious a matter to be left to the politicians."*
>
> *–Charles de Gaulle*

You may have tried to forget it, but I remember Election Day 2000.

For me, the day started in snowy Santa Fe, New Mexico, where I had spent the week working with several community groups. By the time election returns started to come in, I was in the airport, waiting for my flight home to San Francisco. My fellow travelers and I watched the results roll in, state by state.

As I boarded my flight, Gore had won Florida.

When we landed an hour and a half later, Bush had Florida.

By the time the airport shuttle dropped me off at my front door, Gore had it back.

When I finally surrendered to electoral exhaustion and went to bed at 1 a.m. that night, Bush had Florida. The rest, of course, was Supreme Court history.

Watching CNN that night was like watching a Ping-Pong match.

That's when I realized it: I was watching. An observer. Sure, I had cast my absentee ballot, but I knew at that moment that my vote was hardly the full-throated holler of all I had to say about our country, my community, and my ideas about how to improve them both. There is a full range of ways to be heard when it comes to the issues we care about, and this book is for those who know that a full-throated voice is just as powerful—and just as necessary—as a vote in American politics.

If we want to use our voices to echo the value of civic participation in American democracy, we need to be smart about keeping the issues in the news, in the candidates' mouths, and in the minds and hearts of our fellow Americans. 2004 is critical to the issues many Americans care about most—the health of the economy and environment, how we keep our families safe in a post-9/11 world, the rights of people who come to this country in search of something better for their families, care for our seniors, and the future of Social Security as a generation of baby boomers begins to dream about retirement.

"Fear of an IRS audit, no matter how unlikely, has deprived many nonprofits of their voice and has hurt the very constituencies that they intend to serve."

—Jeffrey Berry, *Tufts University Professor of Political Science, Washington Post (11/30/03)*

For far too long, savvy community-based groups have watched from the sidelines through election cycle after election cycle, having little say in policy outcomes and doing little to ensure elected officials will work on behalf of community interests. We then spend the rest of the year trying to influence policy we had no hand in setting and sway decision makers we had no hand in seating. It's a recipe for marginalization that many community groups seem to duplicate election year after election year. Even some of the most sophisticated nonprofits hesitate to engage in advocacy for fear of jeopardizing their nonprofit status.

What's really in jeopardy are the issues we care about most. Voter education and mobi-

lization are no longer luxuries for social change groups—the future of our communities depends on our engagement in the political process. Civic engagement is not separate from the work—it *is* the work.

Election years provide us with a ready-made media-covered event. We can use them to raise the profile of your issues, educate people about a candidate's record, get the candidates on the record, and get incumbents to actually move your agenda and advance your policy goals.

"If you are not engaging in the electoral arena, you are not relevant."

—Rob McKay, *President, McKay Foundation*

For all these reasons, this political moment demands this book. Now is the time for community advocates, nonprofit groups, and everyone who cares about American democracy to get informed and get engaged. Nonprofit groups need to know how they can effectively and legally advocate on behalf of their issues and their constituents in this election year. This book is designed to help your nonprofit organization take advantage of election-year opportunities and give you real tools, tactics, and techniques to make your voice heard and your issues count in 2004.

"Communication is central to effective advocacy.... We need communications strategies to reach, educate and persuade external audiences, from policy makers to communities."

—Lisa VeneKlasen and Valerie Miller, *A New Weave of People, Power and Politics*

WHAT IS THE SPIN PROJECT?

The SPIN Project is a nonprofit group of communications specialists who provide capacity-building to nonprofit public-interest organizations across the nation. SPIN helps organizations increase their effectiveness in influencing debate, shaping public opinion, and garnering positive media attention. We are increasing the capacity of organizations to get their voices heard and to do more effective media work on issues important to the future of our society. SPIN offers public relations consulting, including comprehensive media training and intensive media strategizing and coaching.

SPIN stands for Strategic Press Information Network. We believe that now is the time for organizations to boldly engage the press, communicate their values, and frame their issues. We seek a stronger democracy in which people enhance and actively participate in the public discourse.

The SPIN Project works with a broad range of social policy, advocacy, and grassroots organizations, all of which are working to strengthen both democracy and public participation. These organizations typically focus on issues concerning civil rights, human rights, social justice, and the environment. The SPIN Project honors the multiracial, multicultural, diverse constituencies of the groups we train. We consistently work with people from a wide range of ages, sexual orientations, ethnicities, and incomes.

We travel widely, training and strategizing with organizations in the field. Our work has taken us from barrios to boardrooms, from Native American reservations to national activist conferences in major U.S. cities.

We invite you to visit our Web site at www.spinproject.org and contact us if you would like to discuss our services.

The SPIN Project was created in January 1997 as a program of the Independent Media Institute (IMI). Our sister program at IMI is AlterNet.org, an online magazine providing a mix of news, opinion, and investigative journalism on subjects ranging from the environment, the drug war, technology, and cultural trends to policy debate, sexual politics, and health. You can see AlterNet articles and ideas peppered throughout this book, and find them online at www.AlterNet.org.

SPIN Project
Independent Media Institute
77 Federal Street
San Francisco, CA 94107
(415) 294-1420
E-mail: info@spinproject.org

NAVIGATING THIS BOOK

This book is designed to support your organization's communication and advocacy work. It is an activist-friendly collection of best practices to help your organization build a good foundation for increasing your capacity for effective communications. In particular, it is meant to help you take advantage of media opportunities presented by the 2004 elections.

We offer concrete, grassroots-friendly solutions and strategies to confront the 2004 political challenge, using communications as a tool to advocate on behalf of your issues and constituents. Case studies, tip sheets, checklists, models, and other tools are here to help you make the information real and practical for your own situation. Contri-butors share their experiences in the spirit of peer mentoring and resource sharing.

What This Book Is *Not*

This publication is not the election-law "bible." While accurate according to our understanding of permissible nonprofit activities under current election law, it is worth noting that the Federal Elections Commission was debating this very matter as we went to press. The landscape is changing quickly, so we highly encourage you to contact legal counsel if you have a question about the legality of your organization's activities. You can direct those questions to the Alliance for Justice at 202-822-6070 or www.afj.org.

While this book is fairly compre-hensive, it's not exhaustive—there's always room for one more case study, one more model and example. There's a host of smart work happening in 2004—voter registration, get-out-the vote drives—as well as an abundance of issue-based work. For more information, contact National Voice at www.nationalvoice.org. They are a coalition of nonprofit and community groups working to maximize public participation in our nation's democratic process.

Sections

The book is divided into seven sections. Pick and choose the information you need and build from the lessons of each section.

Section One: The Political Moment offers a bird's-eye view of the 2004 political landscape and the role nonprofits have to play.

Section Two: Know the Law, Don't Fear It reviews the realities of election law for nonprofits. Just the facts!

Section Three: Framing a Progressive Agenda offers concepts and case studies to help you communicate your issues in ways that will resonate with voters and community members.

Section Four: Moving Your Message in the Elections Cycle gives you information to integrate smart strategies into your 2004 plans—including an overview of the election-year news cycle—and to help you maximize opportunities to educate the public about your issues. This section also provides a comprehensive survey of numerous media tactics you can use in an election year, ranging from releasing reports to hosting candidates' forums.

Section Five: Emerging Strategies reviews some of the latest communications trends and offers tips on how to put these new strategies to work for your organization.

Section Six: Critical Constituencies provides ideas on how to engage your base—and beyond—for the 2004 election cycle. It emphasizes the important roles of communities of color, people of faith, and youth.

Section Seven: Resources points you toward more help and information.

Who Is This Book For? How Can It Help You?

Engaging in progressive, proactive media work requires a significant commitment of an organization's resources and usually a step up in its public profile. This is especially true for groups and activists in campaign mode: high-pressure, time-constrained media "war room" situations. This book is designed to assist both national and grassroots organizations to maximize their media potential.

This book was prepared primarily with grassroots groups in mind. However, its information and lessons are completely transferable to just about any social change organization working at the local, state, regional, and even national level.

Loud and Clear in an Election Year: Amplifying the Voices of Community Advocates is for activists and organizations who:

- Want to integrate media work into other campaign activities, including organizing, research, policy, advocacy, lobbying, fundraising, and public education. We do not see media as standing outside those activities, but as integral to the overall work.

- Want to engage their members and highlight their issues in the 2004 elections. This book is for groups who need to be heard, to shape public policy, and to become powerful players in community politics.

- View the election as an opportunity to catalyze and amplify their broader social change efforts.

- Can absorb intensified media scrutiny and responsibilities. We presume if you are

ready to engage in meaningful communications advocacy, you have the organizational infrastructure and financial and staff resources to sustain such an effort. If not, you might want to focus on organizational development before engaging in proactive media work.

- Want to work *with* the media, not *against* it. Although opposition to issues and ideas often comes in the form of editorial opinions by daily newspapers or hot-head radio and TV personalities—and despite the frustration this causes—this book is designed to give you resources and skills to engage the media in a fair and respectful manner. This book is for those who believe in treating journalists with professional respect, and in being a resource for—not an obstacle to—reporters.

- Get a "buzz" from spinning. If you understand how reporters do their jobs, how they think, what their editors demand, and how news is made, you can do a better job spinning your message.

- Have news to make. Don't waste reporters' time with non-news. Have a story to tell; be newsworthy.

- Have a limited budget for advertising campaigns, PR consultants, focus group or polling research, and other costly activities. Although those activities are important and should be considered strongly and budgeted for if possible, you won't need a lot of money to do many of the tactics suggested in this book. You will need *some* money and in several cases even *significant* financial resources, so plan accordingly.

- Believe media work requires planning. We suggest reality-based tactics. We also present the rich range of possibilities. Ultimately, however, it is up to you to decide what is realistic and doable for your campaign.

- Understand there is no "magic silver bullet" solution, frame, message, or tactic. It is never possible to predict precisely what will work or not when it comes to PR. Even the best plans can flop. Don't take it personally. Find what works for you and do it.

Section I

THE POLITICAL
MOMENT

Now is the time to be seen and heard, not the time to duck for cover. Fact is, election years provide an excellent backdrop and stage for your education and advocacy work. Decision makers, the media, your members, clientele, constituencies, and even donors are paying closer attention because it's an election year.

Here's where you can learn how to seize the opportunity for your nonprofit to do more in 2004: showcase your work in the media, build grassroots power, and conduct voter registration and mobilization.

Photo: Election officials in Palm Beach County, Florida, examine punchcard ballots from the questionable pile during a countywide hand recount of presedential ballots on November 17, 2000.

NAACP VOTER Registration DRIVE....

Photo: Library of Congress

ELECTION-YEAR OPPORTUNITIES

By Kim Haddow

Election years traditionally send charitable nonprofits—501(c)(3)s whose donors can deduct their gifts for tax purposes—scurrying for cover. They fear that media coverage of the public education and advocacy work they do during the election year will be misread as electioneering that helps or harms one candidate or party and could endanger their tax status.

But an election year is not the time to disappear. In fact, it is a good time to showcase issues, to be seen and heard, and to heighten an organization's profile and influence at a time when policy makers, politicians, the media, and the public are all paying attention to issues, not just candidates. An election year is an 11-month opportunity to do the following types of important work for your issue:

- Leverage the political process for maximum impact and exposure

- Engage and encourage candidates to address your agenda and your issues

- Get the candidates on the record

- Persuade them to change, or, if a challenger, to adopt your position

- Educate people about the candidates' records

- Receive media coverage that will help you educate the public, increase your profile and influence, and reassure donors that you haven't disappeared

Why Aren't Nonprofits Seizing Election-Year Opportunities?

If elections provide so many opportunities and such a useful backdrop, why have nonprofits been so hesitant to take advantage of the spotlight? According to Tufts University political science professor Jeffrey Berry, it's because most 501(c)(3) organizations don't understand tax law or where the line is between permissible and illegal activity.

Berry, who surveyed more than 1,700 tax-deductible nonprofits drawn randomly from IRS records, reported his findings in a *Washington Post* opinion piece entitled, "The Lobbying Law Is More Charitable than They Think" (11/30/03):

> We found that the typical executive director of a 501(c)(3) has little understanding of what the law actually says. Almost half of those surveyed are so ignorant of the law that they don't even believe their organization has the right to take a public stand on federal legislation (perfectly permissible), while 45 percent believe they are not allowed to sponsor a debate featuring candidates running for public office (they can't support a candidate, but a candidate forum is just fine).

Photo: Peter Holderness

The fact that most nonprofits shy away from doing all the law allows has real costs and consequences, according to Berry. He believes nonprofits "play a special role in American society, and that role is growing. They are often closer to the problems—and the solutions—than the policy makers in city halls, state capitols, and Washington." There's no one to bring this particular perspective into play if you sit out the election year.

501(c)(3)s Must Do More in 2004

Elections are the only regularly scheduled and structured events that allow our society to review and assess local and national policy and direction. Clearly, nonprofits have a unique and necessary voice in the public debate and can and must be heard during elections.

The nature and means of civic and political communications are changing in ways that benefit organizations operating at the grassroots level and that have real and longtime connections to the community. Candidates and advocacy groups are relying less on paid media to educate and persuade and more on one-on-one, person-to-person contact to spread the word. Part of the reason for the shift comes from reforms in campaign finance laws limiting broadcast advertising by some advocacy groups during elections. Beyond that, broadly cast communications are increasingly seen as background noise that clutters the airwaves. More important, they are also becoming less trusted.

Americans are actively seeking other information sources. According to a Pew Research Center poll released in January 2004, one-third of Americans now get their political information from the Internet. The survey also found that Americans are turning away from establishment media and toward new and unconventional outlets for information, such as Jon Stewart's *Daily Show* broadcast on cable TV's Comedy Channel.

Americans receive at least 8,000 messages a day—some estimate upwards of 60,000 or more a week—communicated through television, radio, magazines, newspaper, e-mail, the Internet, and signage. Because they cannot possibly absorb all this information, people are finding trusted filters to help them sort through the barrage and determine what information has value for them.

ELECTION 2004 TRENDS PLAY TO OUR STRENGTHS

Information-delivery mechanisms are different this year—and those differences provide grassroots nonprofits with advantages that help them get the word out.

There will be less television and radio advertising this year, particularly in the fall. Not only do the new federal campaign reform laws prohibit TV and radio advertising by issue advocacy groups within 30 days of a primary election and 60 days of a general election, but communicators have become convinced that the barrage of ads at the end of the 2002 elections overwhelmed, confused, or disgusted voters. That means issue advocates and political campaigns will be resorting to more retail, one-to-one communications and depending less on wholesale, broadly cast outreach.

There will be an emphasis on working with and through local and trusted organizations that already have people networks in place and know how to communicate at the grassroots level. Since 9/11, Americans have felt less able to control the world and more able to affect only what is near and dear. Family and community have become more important, and groups that are helping protect local people and tackling problems at the local level have increased traction and trust.

Use of the Internet as a community action tool is increasing. It is one more way that Americans are filtering the information they allow into their daily lives. It can also be a very intimate and personal way to communicate with people who opt-in, who choose to hear more from you. Using e-mail and the Web to educate and encourage action is inexpensive and, if done right (without spamming), quite effective. Consider it another form of one-on-one, person-to-person communications worth investing in.

More and more organizations are finding ways to highlight their issues this election year. You won't be alone in the wilderness. More 501(c)(3)s are planning to do more this year and more groups than ever have created parallel organizations with 501(c)(4) status, which allows them to participate directly in the election using independent expenditure campaigns. And some of those groups are creating affiliates with 527 IRS status, which allows them to do hard-hitting, partisan advocacy.

Bottom line: more issue groups are carving out roles for themselves and ensuring their voices will be heard in 2004.

Hence the rise of viral e-mail passed from friend to friend or from one member of a virtual community to another. People are more likely to open and believe the e-mail they receive from their friends, family, and fellow members of their church, club, or cause organizations.

Grassroots organizations that already have a respected profile in the community, that are known as players working locally and close to home on backyard issues, and that have a "people network" in place have a real advantage as trusted navigators, communicators, and truth-tellers.

Now more than ever, it is time for nonprofits to seize the opportunities provided by elections to educate and communicate their issues beyond their own constituencies.

What Can Nonprofits Do During the Election Year?

Tax-deductible nonprofits can engage in a spate of election-year activities—so long as they do not endorse or contribute funds to a candidate and do not favor one party, candidate or group of candidates over another. The following are all permissible activities, if they are conducted on a nonpartisan basis, as defined in IRS guidance:

- Registering voters

- Sponsoring candidate forums and debates

- Educating candidates on issues

- Issuing legislative scorecards and report cards

- Educating and training the public and media—issuing voter guides informing voters of candidates' records and positions, conducting polling and survey work and releasing results to the public

- Obtaining candidate position statements on questionnaires

- Sponsoring and campaigning on ballot initiatives

What Charitable Nonprofits Cannot Do:

- Endorse or oppose a candidate or political party

- Contribute money to a candidate or political party

- Display any bias for or against a candidate or political party

- Question an individual about his or her candidate or political party preference during voter registration

Photo: David Bacon

Practical Suggestions for Using Elections to Advance Your Nonprofit's Message

By Kim Haddow, with thanks to Fenton Communications

1. Understand the benchmarks of the election cycle.

Timing is everything. Knowing when the media are paying attention, when most of the public tunes in (after Labor Day), when policy makers are most susceptible to pressure and eager for public praise will all help you maximize media attention and stay legal. (For a broader discussion of these opportunities, see "Election Cycle Benchmarks" in Section 4 of this book.)

2. Stay legal.

Make a member of your staff the "compliance officer," charged with knowing the state and federal laws that apply to your organization. Get good information about the laws and current FEC rulings, which were changing even as we went to press with this book.

Recognize, both for legal reasons and to enhance the effectiveness of your organization's communications, that an election year is *not* the time to introduce new issues or advocacy campaigns. Heighten the profile of the issues you have been working on that already have public and media recognition. Your track record with these issues will bring you more credibility and standing with the media as you seek additional coverage. Sticking with the issues you traditionally work on is also less likely to draw legal scrutiny: Feeding a fire that's already burning is less likely to draw attention than starting a new blaze.

3. Map out the year.

Understand how politicians use the legislative session for positioning, or jockeying for media coverage. Mark immovable dates on your calendars: the petition-gathering period, deadlines for filing and qualifying for candidacy, primary and general election dates, dates of the major party conventions, Labor Day. Look for and plan to exploit traditional events such as candidates' announcement tours, debates, and forums, advertising flights (when new ads hit the airwaves), and retail campaigning (candidate rallies, door knocking, visits to day care and senior centers, etc.). Be sensitive to the year's traditional events and cycles, including religious holidays; secular holidays such as Earth Day, Mother's Day, and Memorial Day; big sporting events such as the World Series and Super Bowl. Pay special attention to the school calendar—people are not likely to show up at a rally if school's out and they're away on vacation.

Figure out how to use the calendar to your advantage either by piggybacking onto a planned event or exploiting a lull in the established schedule when you could create an event that captures the attention of candidates, media, and the public. If you use these cycles, ride 'em and don't try to buck them; getting more media coverage will be easier.

4. Monitor the media.

You should already know who in the media covers your issues in the legislature, but during election seasons many newsrooms restructure to accommodate the heavier news cycle. Find out which reporters are covering the elections and build relationships with them that enable you to feed stories that take advantage of the candidates and their election activities to spotlight your issues.

5. Make sure your position is understood.

Prepare materials and brief the media and the public on your issue and stance. Be clear—and vocal—about your priorities and proposed solutions.

6. Generate coverage.

In 2004, the inside baseball of the presidential elections will get plenty of ink and airtime. Very little media time will go to covering where state and local candidates stand on specific issues. But you can use a number of tools to increase coverage and get the record out.

- *Legislative scorecards.* Releasing and scoring an officeholder's voting record gives the media and public a clear understanding of the candidate's history on your issue. It is safest to score the entire delegation or regional delegation, not just incumbents who are running for reelection.

- *Report cards.* Comparing and contrasting track records and quoting candidate statements allows challengers to be included based on what's been said and done, but must not include an endorsement, be partisan, or exclude any candidate running for the office.

- *Questionnaires.* If you can get candidates to respond, questionnaires require them to go beyond the general to the specific. When done, you have results you can release to the media.

Engage candidates. Invite candidates and the media to tour the local polluting power plant or overcrowded health care clinic. You may take them individually, but you must invite them all, and invite the media each time.

Engage the public. Build a community around your issue—use house parties, video screenings, door-to-door canvassing, and literature drops to recruit volunteers and do public education. The press will get educated, too—if you invite them to come along.

7. Get in the picture.

Show up where the candidates show up. Get their public appearance schedule on the Internet and determine whether reporters are likely to cover the event. Deploy a squad of members to appear up front at each location—with nonpartisan signs. Make sure your folks are easily identifiable and are either dressed in matching (nonpartisan) T-shirts or are accompanied by props that attract the camera's eye. For example, an inflatable smokestack could herald the need for action on clean air.

8. Flush 'em out.

Ask questions at town meetings and plant questions with reporters. If candidates refuse to meet or discuss issues, publicize the fact. Don't be afraid to use materials like flyers, paid advertising, or billboards to broadcast candidates' stands or reveal their unwillingness to take a stand on your issue.

9. Promote editorials.

Engage editorial boards by submitting letters outlining the candidates' positions and your expertise. Offer to meet with the editorial staff for a briefing. Make sure to keep sending letters to the editor—they make an impression on the public and the editorial staff.

10. Plan events.

Prepare for convention and other political party gatherings. Party meetings at county and state levels are opportunities to generate coverage. The meetings are largely staged, with lots of downtime and little real news value, but the audience is important and full of influential people. For a nonprofit, there are limits on what you can do, so get good information on the law. And know that the law doesn't limit you from the following activities:

- Setting up an information booth

- Handing out a clever lapel pin or other memorable material

- Staging a media event

- Flooding hotels where delegates are staying with materials

- Advertising in convention programs

BUILDING GRASSROOTS POWER

By Dan Petagorsky

All across the country, community-based groups are using the political system to build grassroots power for traditionally marginalized constituencies and progressive issues. In the West, organizers are engaging first-time Native American and Latino voters in school board and legislative races and in ballot issues centering on economic justice and civil rights. In Oregon, a dozen years of organizing against anti-gay attacks has helped the state's gay rights movement build a broad resource bank of skills, supportive voters, allies, donors, and volunteers. In Washington state, organized labor and community-based allies won a ballot measure indexing the minimum wage to the cost of living, and in Nevada they succeeded in winning multilingual worker-safety training. These examples are only the beginning.

The election season presents a wide range of opportunities for building grassroots power, from holding candidate forums and publishing research on your issue to participating in initiative campaigns. The group I work with, the Western States Center, trains and encourages groups to recognize and capitalize on the full range of possibilities for your organization or community to engage in and build power through civic engagement.

Movement-Building for Power

The progressive movement can use the election year to build power for communities that are often left out of the political debate. By joining election year activities with the values-based goals of ongoing community organizing, we can build power to advance social and economic justice. Here's what a "movement-building" campaign can do for your group:

- Bring more people on board and expand your base of members, donors, volunteers and supporters

- Mobilize and energize these people

- Develop new leaders and greater organizing capacity

- Influence or control the terms of public debate by developing winning, value-based messages

- Hold elected officials accountable

- Move a long-term progressive agenda

- Win concrete improvements in people's lives

Organizing to Shift Power

At the same time, the political system is part of the dominant structure that continues to disenfranchise whole classes of people. Its promise remains unfulfilled as long as the flow of money and other barriers limit participation along lines of race, class, and gender. Changing the way our political system works—fulfilling the true promise of democracy—requires work on two parallel tracks:

- Organizing to remove barriers to equal access and full participation. Strategies for working within the current electoral system should reflect an understanding of the limitations of that system and should seek to challenge those barriers whenever possible.

- Building grassroots power through grassroots organizing. Many in this country don't have political power— poor and working-class people, people of color, women, youth, religious and sexual minorities, and others who don't fit the mainstream norm. Taking up space in the political process, organizing to move the issues, voicing a message that challenges corporate domination— these are steps toward political power.

Dan Petagorsky is Executive Director of the Western States Center in Portland, Oregon. Western States Center's mission is to build a progressive movement for social, economic, racial, and environmental justice in the eight Western states of Oregon, Washington, Idaho, Montana, Wyoming, Utah, Nevada and Alaska.

WINNING MUCH MORE THAN VOTES

From Californians for Justice, founded in 1996 to build power in communities of color across California

While candidate campaigns have a sole goal of winning by 50 percent plus one vote on Election Day, movement-building campaigns have some very different, nonpartisan goals: to build power and create lasting social change. Nonetheless, you can use the election year as an opportunity to build toward your larger, long-term goals. Here are some of the activities a movement-building campaign could engage in within an election year context:

- Educate the public on issues that advance longer-term progressive goals.

- Expand the base of people involved in the political process—and in campaign leadership. Recruit and train effective grassroots leaders to make decisions about strategy and campaign direction, as well as to register voters and get out the vote on Election Day. The campaign empowers the constituency.

- Develop winning, values-based messages on issues in the forefront of the campaign. At a minimum, a powerful movement-building campaign message does no harm to other communities and constituencies; at its best, the message educates and moves the public to action on the issue.

- Work with constituents to develop a political analysis and the skills necessary to advance a political agenda.

- Gain power for disenfranchised constituencies.

- Build community organizations and leaders by helping them gain experience in specific arenas, such as coalition work, field organizing, message discipline, and so forth.

- Recognize that resources used in the campaign are viewed as a long-term investment in the goals of the community.

Balancing the goals of an immediate win—on a ballot initiative, for example—and long-term movement-building is a challenge. Being clear about our goals and bottom lines is critical. Keep your eyes on the prize and remember that elections are a means, not an end, to a stronger progressive movement.

Why Should Communities and Community Organizations Care About Elections?

Here are a few reasons for community-based organizations to get involved in election-year activities:

1. Power

Active, organized participation in an election year can give community groups a lot of power. When a community group gets organized enough to have a voice in our democracy, it becomes a force that politicians have to pay attention to. When you turn out large numbers of voters, you build political power.

2. Legitimacy

When your organization works successfully in the democratic process, people with power treat your organization with respect. (This is especially true when you combine your election-year work with other kinds of organizing.)

3. Organization and coalition-building

The valuable discipline and skills people learn in an election-year can be transferred to other kinds of non-election year activities, like community organizing and grassroots education. The experience of working successfully in coalition with other community groups on a concrete, time-limited project like getting out the vote can make it easier to collaborate on other joint projects.

CASE STUDY

TURNING OUT YOUR BASE

By Joanne Wright and Zach Polett

ACORN, the Association of Community Organizations for Reform Now, is a neighborhood-based organization that represents the interests of low-to-moderate-income families and their communities.

Back in the early 1980s, as ACORN was just starting its second decade, a group of ACORN leaders from Arkansas held a meeting with then-Senator Dale Bumpers to get his support on some affordable housing legislation. We got some good news and some bad news from Senator Bumpers that day. The good news was that he said he agreed with us and would be supporting the legislation. The bad news was that he told us that it wouldn't pass. And the reason it wouldn't pass, he explained, was that each of his colleagues in both houses of Congress knew full well who voted and who didn't vote in their districts and states and that poor people, those who most cared about affordable housing, weren't registered in high numbers and didn't vote. And he was right: We got his support and the legislation didn't pass. But we also learned a valuable lesson: If we don't register, educate, and turn out our communities to vote, we will continue to be marginalized in the public policy decisions that affect our members' lives.

So for ACORN, registering the residents of ACORN neighborhoods to vote and then motivating these neighbors to vote around the issues that are important to our communities—affordable housing, income distribution, access to health care, quality public education, and so forth—are a critical part of our everyday mission and work.

As we approach a presidential election year in which the concerns of low- and moderate-income people are not on the nation's agenda, ACORN has a strategy for increasing voter registration and voter turnout in low-income African-American and Latino communities. It focuses on using strong, nonpartisan messages about issues that matter to people in those communities to mobilize new and existing voters.

Over the years we've learned that voter turnout projects are more effective when they occur under the auspices of an existing community organization with trusted mem-

Photo: Peter Holdnerness

Local community activists from ACORN in Phoenix, Arizona, welcome workers from California en route to DC on the Immigrant Workers Freedom Ride.

bers and a track record on issues that matter to voters. With a member on every block and a proven record of organizing people to fight for and win real change, ACORN is that community organization in the 700 communities in 60 cities where we work.

For 34 years, ACORN members have been at the forefront of voter participation work in low- and moderate-income communities. In the 2001–2002 election cycle, ACORN chapters in 23 states registered 216,248 voters, then contacted more than 1 million occasional voters and new registrants in targeted precincts to urge them to vote on Election Day.

For 2004, our voter participation efforts consist of developing community-based organi-zational infrastructure, voter registration, and comprehensive voter contact and mobiliza-tion work.

Building Infrastructure

When we mount large voter turnout pro-grams, we make an investment in building the infrastructure of the organization that will pay off for years to come. ACORN builds community networks of trained activists with practical organizing skills who can mobilize other residents in future issue-based and voter turnout campaigns. By par-ticipating in voter mobilization work in an election year, members get a civic education that connects to their year-round issue cam-paign work, such as working to increase the supply of affordable housing.

VOTER REGISTRATION TIPS

If you want to register your organization's members or community allies, here are a few tips to dramatically improve your results:

Avoid Yes/No questions.

Instead of a yes/no question such as, "Are you registered to vote?," engage potential registrants on issues that matter. For example, you could say, "Hi, my name is Pat, and I'm here registering people to vote because I want politicians who'll improve the quality of our schools." (Educate volunteers that they may not highlight issues that are wedge issues between candidates.) Then ask, "What's your last name?" Using a blank registration card, fill in the person's last name for them, then hand them the card on a clipboard and move on to the next person.

Ask follow-up questions.

If someone tells you they are already registered to vote, don't stop the conversation there. Ask if they are registered to vote *at their present address*. Ask if they voted in the last presidential election to make sure that they haven't been purged from the voter rolls. If they answer "no" to either question, register them again.

Set goals and track progress daily.

Set goals for how many voter registration cards you plan to collect during each registration session. During and after each session, check in to see how volunteers are progressing toward the goals. Communication is key. If people don't know what they're aiming for and how they're progressing, how can they succeed?

Voter Registration

In most states, Americans can't vote unless they've registered some time before Election Day (a few states allow voter registration on Election Day). ACORN registers hundreds of new voters every day by working "high volume" sites (bus stations, neighborhood grocery stores, community events, social service centers, and the like) and doing door-to-door outreach in targeted precincts with a high concentration of low-income households. Persistent organizers can register four to six voters per hour. Once in hand, every registration card is photocopied before it is submitted. Vital information about each new voter is then entered into a database, essential for subsequently mobilizing new voters to the polls.

Mobilizing Voters with Issue-Based Messages

Because of experiences like those with Senator Bumpers, ACORN members place a high value on delivering voters to the polls once they are registered. ACORN's long history of working in low- and moderate-income communities has taught us that people are most likely to vote if voting is connected to some issue about which they care deeply. Therefore, we use our community networks to take action on issues of importance to our members and to connect those issues to the electoral process.

In the first quarter of each year, we organize annual kick-off meetings in which community residents come together to evaluate the work of the past year and set issue priorities for the new one. This issue platform is key to the work, because as long as elections are seen as separate from the community's priorities, low-income communities will not develop a culture of participation and voting.

Each ACORN chapter then pursues a campaign around the major priorities set at the meeting. The nonpartisan messages we end up using in our 2004 voter turnout program will flow directly from the issue campaign work pursued throughout the year.

Get-Out-the-Vote

The final step in a successful voter mobilization program is an effective Get-Out-the-Vote (GOTV) campaign that targets the new registrants and other voters in ACORN neighborhoods. In 2004, using the nonpartisan issue-based messages, ACORN will carry out an extensive program of door-knocking, house visits, house meetings, and neighborhood meetings and rallies in ACORN neighborhoods, with a goal of boosting overall voter turnout from these communities. We will run three overlapping and complementary voter contact programs, each designed to reinforce the other: ACORN organizer outreach, the political canvass, and the Precinct Leaders Action Plan (PLAN) program.

ACORN Organizer Outreach

ACORN places major emphasis on direct personal contact in our GOTV efforts. ACORN has two to ten full-time field organizers working in targeted neighborhoods. In the four months leading up to Election Day, each ACORN staffer will make about 375 personal contacts per month—half through door knocking, half through house meetings, neighborhood-wide meetings, and events. As they contact ACORN members and other voters about the election, organizers are recruiting precinct leaders who will in turn door-knock their neighbors and get them out to the polls.

Photo: Peter Holderness

Immigrant Worker Freedom Riders from Orlando, Florida, rallied for immigration reform at Liberty State Park in New Jersey en route to the Capitol.

Political Canvass

We also organize crews of paid canvassers for GOTV. Starting six weeks before the election, we go door-to-door six days a week, engaging people in conversations about issues at stake in the election, getting them to commit to voting, asking them to take lawn signs, and leaving behind literature. The week before the election, we revisit these voters with a shorter door-knock interaction, reminding them of the upcoming election and leaving behind more literature. During the week before the election, we make two rounds of calls to our targeted voters and send one or two pieces of GOTV mail.

ACORN Precinct Leader Action Networks

Field organizers recruit and mobilize block captains from our community networks who agree to contact their neighbors about the election. These Precinct Leader Action Networks (PLANs) mobilize ACORN members to visit and call each home in the community about voting. The PLAN block captains educate residents on the issues, ask for a signed "Count on Me" commitment to vote, and then follow up with phone calls and personal visits as election day nears. Each block captain is responsible for contacting 50 voters.

Outcomes

All this time and energy pay off. In the fall of 2002, for example, Rhode Island ACORN built a coalition of diverse community organizations. The group targeted 12 precincts on the South Side of Providence, with a particular focus on Latino neighborhoods. After registering 4,000 new voters, the coalition knocked on 6,000 doors twice over the three weeks prior to the election, and on Election Day called every voter five times and knocked on every door three times. In 1998, the turnout was 3,365. In 2002, it was 4,828, an astounding 42 percent increase.

ACORN members are continually waging campaigns to force politicians to address issues of concern to their communities, such as jobs, education, healthy communities, and immigrant rights. Members are keenly aware that politicians are inclined to reserve their attention for communities that vote on Election Day.

If we are successful in turning out significant numbers of voters in ACORN members' low-income neighborhoods, elected officials will be much more likely to address the issues of concern to low-income communities. As ACORN members and their neighbors see the impact of their actions, they become more likely to continue to participate in American civic life for years to come.

Joanne Wright is Deputy Director for Project Vote, a national nonpartisan voter registration, education and mobilization organization with a 22-year history of delivering voter participation services and training to a wide variety of communities and organizations.

Zach Polett is Director of Political Operations for ACORN and its family of organizations.

CASE STUDY
2002 CAMPAIGN TO
MOBILIZE THE
IMMIGRANT VOTE

By Monica Regan and Maria Rogers Pascual

The Northern California Citizenship Project (NCCP) seized the November 2002 elections as an opportunity to mobilize immigrant voters, strengthen community leaders, and build lasting relationships with constituents. Maximizing scarce resources, NCCP engaged in media advocacy to broaden the impact of its community-based voter education and mobilization campaign.

The Need for a Representative Voting Population

In 2002 California was, as it continues to be, at the leading edge of population change transforming the nation. Our state made headlines as census data revealed that people of color had become a majority. The data also estimated that one in four residents of the state are foreign-born. But despite the demographic shift, the voting population is still far from representative of the population as a whole. Non-Hispanic whites constituted 48 percent of the state population in 2000, but 71 percent of its voters.

At the same time, there were several positive trends: the 1990s saw record numbers of immigrants becoming naturalized citizens.

> "Participating in the outreach campaign was a positive experience that increased [the members'] ability and confidence to do similar work in the future."
>
> *MIV campaign participant*

Though overall voter turnout in the state has steadily declined since the 1970s, the Latino vote, for example, propelled by population growth, increased from 4 percent in 1990 to 14 percent in 2000. Despite the momentum, multiple barriers remain to immigrants' full participation in the democratic process.

To address these barriers, NCCP launched a campaign we called *Mobilize the Immigrant Vote! (MIV)* in July 2002. The goals of the campaign were to increase immigrant participation in the November 2002 general election and to strengthen immigrant community leadership and activism for ongoing work toward social change.

Salon Sihombring, left, and Fransico Herrera entertain Freedom Riders on the bus near Walla Walla, Washington. Photo: Paul T. Erickson/Tri-City Herald

Goals of *Mobilize the Immigrant Vote!*

NCCP works to strengthen democracy and advance social justice by increasing the capacity of community organizations to engage and empower their immigrant constituents. For the MIV 2002 campaign, we partnered with 14 diverse community-based organizations, providing training, technical assistance, mini-grants, and other support to each organization so it could carry out the campaign in its community. To increase voter turnout, MIV partner organizations undertook a variety of voter registration, education, and mobilization activities, including distribution of flyers, phone-banking, and precinct walking. To increase community capacity for ongoing immigrant civic participation and activism, partner organizations recruited and provided leadership-building opportunities for more than 250 community members who participated in campaign activities.

Using the Media to Reach Our Goals

Much of the work in the MIV campaign involved contacting immigrant voters through community-based voter education and mobilization activities. To complement our face-to-face efforts and broaden our impact, we incorporated media advocacy as a central component of the campaign. We aimed to reach large numbers in immigrant communities—potential voters and policy makers alike—about the power and importance of immigrant participation in American democracy.

Our partner organizations represented Latino, Chinese, Vietnamese, Korean, Cambodian, Iranian, and other immigrant communities. To reach the constituencies of these diverse groups, and to increase the overall visibility and credibility of partner organizations' work, we used ethnic media to amplify our message.

Overcoming Challenges to Achieve Our Goals

At the onset of the MIV media campaign, we were met with formidable challenges familiar to many nonprofits: Our staff was over-stretched. We had limited resources. We had a short time frame. Most of our participants had little or no experience in media and communications.

To be strategic with the resources we had, we began by narrowing the types of people we wanted to reach through the media: immigrant communities, political candidates, policy makers, and funders. We identified specific media outlets to reach these target audiences. In collaboration with our partner organizations, we produced a list of 42 ethnic and mainstream outlets in geographic areas where our target audiences were concentrated. We researched reporters who were most likely to cover the topic (such as those who had previously written about citizenship, elections, and California's changing demographics), and we brainstormed effective news hooks.

Pitching Our Story

The newsworthiness of MIV was largely based on the impending November elections. We chose four promising news hooks: the uniqueness of our campaign, the diversity of the groups represented, the human interest angle, and the implications of California's demographic shift.

We created a media packet with a press release, list of MIV campaign activities and spokespeople, and a fact sheet with background and statistics on changing demographics and the importance of the immigrant vote. We also provided media training to all MIV partner organizations, helping them develop and hone their messages and teaching them how to get their activities covered in the media. Finally, we conducted training for spokespeople to ensure that our messengers stayed on message.

Photo: Peter Holderness

FREEDOM

Immigrant
RIGHTS
NOW

AFL-CIO

Developing Our Message

Our message was developed to ensure it represented the collective concerns of our partner organizations. We used the SPIN Project's "Problem-Solution-Action" model to capture action while advocating for a distinct set of values. We asked ourselves: What are we *for*? Whose interests are at stake? What do we want people to do? The message we developed communicated our frame, our position, and our call for action:

Problem—Though the growth of immigrant communities has dramatically changed the face of California, this change is not reflected among voters. Many barriers remain that limit immigrants' full participation.

Solution—We must continue to break down the barriers for immigrants and new citizens so they can use their growing numbers and clout to affect policies and hold leaders accountable. We must take concrete steps to speed the process by which immigrants are organizing and naturalizing.

Action—We call on new citizens to register to vote and turn out on Election Day. Let's bridge the gap between those who vote in California and those who live in California!

Fruits of Our Labor

The media coverage we garnered far exceeded our initial communications goals. We ended up with 15 media hits from the 42 outlets we targeted. Several mainstream media outlets covered our story, including the *San Francisco Chronicle*, the *San Jose Mercury News* and public radio station KQED. Ethnic media outlets also picked up the story, including *Asianweek*, *Sing Tao Daily*, and the television stations Univisión, and Telemundo. As a result, we estimate that the MIV campaign likely informed more than 1 million people about the importance of the immigrant voice and about the work of MIV participating organizations.

Among a sample of registered voters who attended MIV-sponsored voter education events, a substantial 80 percent cast ballots on Election Day.

The media work also helped increase our partner organizations' visibility. One participating organization noted, "The MIV campaign created positive spotlights for our organization. People are starting to take notice. The encouragement has greatly increased staff morale and involvement in issues pertinent to our communities."

The six-month campaign planted seeds for further media work. Seventy-five percent of the organizations that participated reported feeling prepared to communicate with the media about their work after the campaign. For the first time, partner organizations collaborated to coordinate news events, shared written material and translations, tactics and strategies, and tips about reporters.

The MIV campaign contributed to strengthening immigrant civic engagement as well as to increasing public awareness that the immigrants' issues cannot be ignored. Given our success, we're gearing up for 2004.

Note: This case study was based on the evaluation report *Mobilize the Immigrant Vote! Evaluation of Northern California Citizenship Project's Capacity-Building Series and Campaign*, August 2003, by Laura Lanzerotti, LaFrance Associates, as well as other NCCP materials. For access to the full report on MIV 2002, visit NCCP's website at www.immigrantvoice.org.

Monica Regan is Director of Programs and Maria Rogers Pascual is Executive Director of the Northern California Citizenship Project. NCCP works to catalyze immigrant civic participation to strengthen democracy and advance social justice.

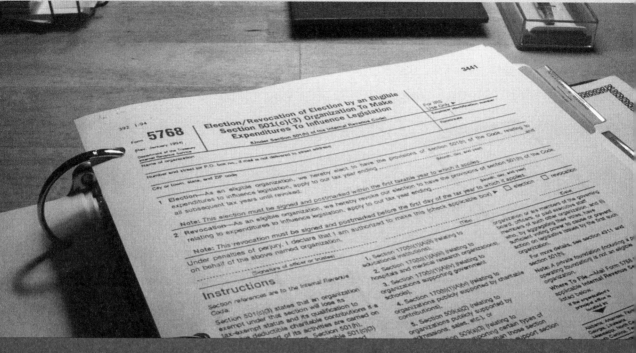

KNOW THE LAW,
DON'T FEAR IT

"Fear of an IRS audit, no matter how unlikely, has deprived many nonprofits of their voice and has hurt the very constituencies that they intend to serve," says Tufts University professor Jeffrey Berry. And he's right—we could and should be doing more. But all of us need to learn what more we are allowed to do by law and what we clearly can't. This section will help you figure out where that line is and how much more you can do in 2004.

990

Return of Organization Ex...

Part I Revenue, Expenses, and Changes in Net Assets or Fund Balances

1a Contributions, gifts, grants...
  b Direct public support
  c Indirect public support
  d Government contributions (grants)
  e Total (add lines 1a through 1d) (cash $ ___ 424,119 noncash $ ___)

		1a	
		1b	
		1c	

2 Program service revenue including government fees and contracts (from Part VII, line 9...) | | 82,729
3 Membership dues and assessments
4 Interest on savings and temporary cash investments
5 Dividends and interest from securities
6a Gross rents
  b Less: rental expenses
  c Net rental income or (loss) (subtract line 6b from line 6a)

| | | 6a | |
| | | 6b | |

7 Other investment income (describe ▲ ___)

	(A) Securities		(B) Other
8a Gross amount from sales of assets other than inventory	2,626	8a	
b Less: cost or other basis and sales expenses	0	8b	
c Gain or (loss) (attach schedule)	2,626	8c	
d Net gain or (loss) (combine line 8c, columns (A) and (B))			8d

9 Special events and activities (attach schedule). **Stmt 1**
  a Gross revenue (not including $ ___ of
    contributions reported on line 1a)

| | 9a | |

  b Less: direct expenses other than fundraising expenses

| | 9b | |

  c Net income or (loss) from special events (subtract line 9b from line 9a) | | | 9c
10a Gross sales of inventory, less returns and allowances

| | 10a | |

  b Less: cost of goods sold

| | 10b | |

  c Gross profit or (loss) from sales of inventory (attach schedule) (subtract line 10b from line 10a) | | | 10c
11 Other revenue (from Part VII, line 103) | | | 11
12 Total revenue (add lines 1e, 2, 3, 4, 5, 6c, 7, 8d, 9c, 10c, and 11) | | | 12

Expenses
13 Program services (from line 44, column (B))
14 Management and general (from line 44, column (C))
15 Fundraising (from line 44, column (A))

POWER, TAX-FREE

By Darci Andresen

The tax-exempt status of your nonprofit organization may not sound like a sexy subject, but many organizations are unclear about how they can participate in the political process. For these groups, even the schlumpy T-shirt method of getting the vote out approaches the status of racy lace underwear.

Nonprofit tax-exempt organizations come in a variety of styles, as indicated by their IRS designations: 501(c)(3), 501(c)(4), and 527. No matter what the style, each carries a certain power in its ability to educate and motivate voters. Election 2004 calls for full-throttle implementation of all of these powers.

Most of the larger organizations, such as the Sierra Club or the National Abortion Rights Action League, have set up both a 501(c)(3) and a 501(c)(4) organization. 501(c)(3)s are meant to educate and edify and are even allowed to do a limited amount of lobbying. For example, they can tell their members to call upon Congress to act on certain pieces of legislation. Off-limits to any 501(c)(3), however, is any level of partisan politicking—no proclamations such as "Bush sucks. Vote for any Democrat who can sit up by themselves." However, 501(c)(3) organizations *can* criticize Bush Administration policies and rate his performance—very carefully.

Even with partisan electioneering benched on the sidelines, a large playing field still exists for 501(c)(3)s to exercise power in the political process by means of conducting voter registration activities, distributing voter education guides, disseminating information about candidates and issues, working on get-out-the-vote drives, hosting candidate debates, and other educational outreach regarding the election itself, democracy, the importance of voting, and so forth. Obviously 501(c)(3) groups should not do anything that may jeopardize their tax-exempt status (see below), but they should boldly implement the tools that *are* at their disposal.

DEFINITIONS

EXPRESS ADVOCACY: Communications that use specific "magic" words like "vote for", "defeat", "reject", etc.

ISSUE ADVOCACY: Nonpartisan communications focusing on issues only, with no call to action—even implied—regarding a candidate.

501(c)(3): An organization exempt from tax under Section 501(c)(3) of the Internal Revenue Code. 501(c)(3)s may engage in some lobbying but may not engage in partisan electoral activity. Contributions to 501(c)(3)s are generally tax-deductible.

501(c)(4): An organization exempt from tax under Section 501(c)(4) of the Internal Revenue Code. 501(c)(4)s may engage in unlimited lobbying and some partisan electoral activity. Contributions to 501(c)(4)s are generally not tax-deductible, and some partisan electioneering activity can subject you to tax.

527: An organization exempt from tax under Section 527 of the Internal Revenue Code as a "political organization." 527 organizations that choose not to engage in "express advocacy" may avoid most disclosure requirements under federal election rules. If they also lack taxable income (by spending it as soon as it is received or by placing money in non-interest-bearing checking accounts), they may avoid some return requirements mandated by the Internal Revenue Code.

POLITICAL ACTION COMMITTEE (PAC): Federal PACs are organizations created with the express goal of affecting the outcome of political elections. Federal PACs can endorse candidates, oppose candidates, and make contributions to candidate campaigns. In many states, PACs may be formed to affect candidate elections or ballot measures, and these state PACs are treated differently for tax purposes.

Photo: David Bacon

Precinct walkers from labor and community organizations prepare for a day of door-knocking in Richmond, California.

More powerful bang for the buck is the 501(c)(4) organization. 501(c)(4)s can conduct unlimited lobbying and can engage in some partisan electoral activity so long as it's not the organization's primary purpose. Although donations to these organizations are not tax-deductible, the organizations themselves are still exempt from most federal taxes.

501(c)(4)s can provide candidate-related information *to their members,* endorse specific candidates, urge the election or defeat of a particular candidate, and encourage contributions to a candidate. The definition of membership is key: Members include people who either pay annual dues to the organization or have a significant attachment to the organization, such as the right to participate in the organization's governance. However, a 501(c)(4) *can* (and *should*) announce its endorsements to the press—an effective way of letting a wider public know of its support.

Although the organization can't coordinate its endorsement with a campaign, the campaign may independently publicize the organization's support. Influential 501(c)(4)s that have name recognition with the public should use this tactic to amplify their power to motivate voters.

There is a specific type of 501(c)(4) organization known as an MCFL-type corporation, which has an ideological mission, is not formed for profit, is tax exempt under Section 501(c)(4) of the Internal Revenue Code and may not accept money from either corporations or unions, just individuals. If these criteria are met, MCFL-type corporations may make independent expenditures for express advocacy communications to the public legally, with FEC reporting. MCFL-type corporations may not make contributions to any candidate campaign, and may not coordinate with any candidate campaign.

Election activities 501(c)(3) organizations can engage in without jeopardizing their tax-exempt status

Nonprofit organizations can engage their communities in 2004. With their large membership bases and extensive networks, nonprofits can educate large numbers of existing and potential voters without jeopardizing their tax-exempt status. The golden rule is simple: All election activities are permissible so long as they do not appear in any way, shape, or form to promote or critique any one candidate.

Much of what can be done within this rule is common sense. But there are many gray areas that may or may not bring scrutiny to the organization depending on what you do, when and how you do it, what you say, to whom, and so forth. Call on resources like the Alliance for Justice to clarify the details of your organization's planned activities.

Federal tax law and state and federal election laws cover these issues. Nonprofits should adhere first to federal tax law, because it often dictates a higher standard than state and federal election law. 501(c)(4) and 527 organizations should pay careful attention to the rules of the Bipartisan Campaign Reform Act, which are in flux even in the midst of the 2004 election cycle.

The following specifies what activities are permissible for 501(c)(3) organizations. Follow the colors to determine how your favorite 501(c)(3) organization can help make Election 2004 a victory for democracy.

Red: Don't Do It

- Endorse candidates.

- Contribute funds to candidates.

- Use organization resources or staff time for candidate election activities (ballot measures are OK, subject to lobbying limits).

- Provide mailing lists to candidates for free or below market-rate.

- Solicit candidate pledges: Nonprofit organizations cannot ask a candidate to pledge to do or not to do something in their campaign or in their eventual election. This provides implicit endorsement and is illegal.

Yellow: Proceed with Caution

- Distribute, post on Web sites, and send out on listservs voter education guides and legislative voting records that address a wide range of issues. Scorecards are not permissible if they indicate that a candidate's position is either "good" or "bad."

- Educate the public on issues as long as the information does not implicitly suggest that people should vote for a particular candidate.

- Educate the public on candidates as long as information is presented on all candidates and on a wide range of issues and without trying to cast candidates in a favorable or unfavorable light. Web sites of 501(c)(3)s may link to the Web sites of all candidates in a race for educational purposes following these guidelines.

- Seek to influence party platforms, as long as you do it for all major parties equally.

Photo: David Bacon

Green: Do it!

Note: All green activities are really chartreuse because there are times when their permissibility is suspect. Check the Bipartisan Campaign Reform Act for the new rules.

- Register people to vote as long as there is no targeting of districts based on partisan demographics, targeting of swing or battleground districts—i.e. you cannot target a "Democratic" area but you can target underrepresented communities, such as African Americans, Latinos, etc.

- Run a get-out-the-vote (GOTV) drive. The same targeting rules apply; see above.

- Host a candidate forum. Make sure all candidates are invited, rules are fair, and the audience is not stacked.

- Candidate questioning. Organizations can encourage their members to ask all the candidates in a race the same (not loaded) question about a particular issue of concern to them. Groups can also continue to criticize public officials who they feel are detrimental to their issues—even when that official is a candidate—if this is an activity the organization also does in the same manner and scope in a non-election year.

- Educate the public via earned media coverage of your issue. Use public education tools such as nonpartisan reports, opinion editorials, and letters to the editor to get the word out about your issue.

- Direct public education about your issue by way of scorecards, Internet communications, door-knocking, and so forth. All of these must be nonpartisan.

- Ballot initiatives are also a tool to make proactive public policy on your issue.

Darci Andresen is the Associate Publisher of AlterNet.org, an online magazine providing a mix of news, opinion, and investigative journalism on subjects ranging from the environment, the drug war, technology, and cultural trends to policy debate, sexual politics, and health.

PERMISSIBLE ELECTION ACTIVITIES CHECKLIST

From the Alliance for Justice

501(c)(3) public charity organizations are strictly forbidden from engaging in any political activity in support of, or in opposition to, any candidate for public office. The IRS will consider all of the facts and circumstances surrounding an activity to determine whether the activity violates this prohibition. Nonetheless, 501(c)(3) public charity organizations *can* engage in nonpartisan voter education activity and in a limited amount of lobbying.

501(c)(3)s *may:*

☐ Engage in limited lobbying, including work on ballot measures

☐ Conduct nonpartisan public education and training sessions about participation in the political process

☐ Educate all of the candidates on public interest issues

☐ Publish legislative scorecards (with certain restrictions)

☐ Prepare candidate questionnaires and create voter guides (with certain restrictions)

☐ Canvass the public on issues

☐ Sponsor candidate debates (with certain restrictions)

☐ Rent, at fair-market value, mailing lists and facilities to other organizations, legislators, and candidates (with certain restrictions)

☐ Conduct nonpartisan get-out-the-vote and voter registration drives

☐ Establish a controlled 501(c)(4) organization

☐ Work with all political parties to get its positions included on the party's platform (with certain restrictions)

501(c)(3)s *may not:*

☐ Endorse candidates for public office

☐ Make any campaign contributions

☐ Make expenditures on behalf of candidates

☐ Restrict rental of their mailing lists and facilities to certain candidates

☐ Ask candidates to sign pledges on any issue (tacit endorsement)

☐ Increase the volume or amount of incumbent criticism as election time approaches

☐ Publish or communicate anything that explicitly or implicitly favors or opposes a candidate

ELECTION ACTIVITIES OF INDIVIDUALS ASSOCIATED WITH 501(C)(3) ORGANIZATIONS

From the Alliance for Justice

Officers, directors, or employees of a 501(c)(3) organization are not prohibited from partisan political campaign activity when they are acting in their individual capacity. Staff may work on political campaigns outside work hours or using their available leave time. However, leaders and volunteers may not use the facilities, equipment, personnel, or other resources of the organization to provide support to or oppose a candidate or campaign.

Following are examples of instances when the actions of board members, officers, or employees can be seen as actions on behalf of the organization in a political campaign.

These types of actions should be avoided:

□ The director of an organization makes statements biased for or against candidates for public office during an event sponsored by the organization or in any of its publications.

□ An employee of an organization wears a political button at a public event or function when acting on behalf of the organization.

□ An employee gives the organization's mailing list to a candidate.

□ An organization permits a candidate to use the organization's office for a phone bank without charge.

□ A board of directors thanks an executive director for her work on behalf of a candidate.

An organization can help to protect itself from violating these laws in the following ways:

□ Requiring officers or employees acting as individuals engaged in partisan political activity to clearly state that they are acting in their individual capacity, not on behalf of the organization, and that any reference to their work for the organization is made only for identification purposes.

□ Notifying employees of the limitation on use of their staff time and office facilities. Timesheets should reflect that an employee took leave to participate in partisan activity.

□ Disavowing any partisan actions of officials or employees that appear to be authorized by the organization and taking steps to ensure such actions are not repeated. Such a disavowal should be in writing and done in a timely manner.

The Alliance for Justice is a national association of advocacy organizations concerned with the environment, civil rights, mental health, and women and children. They also offer a technical assistance hotline to nonprofits, and you can call them at 866-NPLOBBY, (866-675-6229). Just ask for Nonprofit Advocacy technical assistance, and they'll put you in touch with an expert who can address questions about your election-year activities. .

TAX-EXEMPT ORGANIZATIONS AND CAMPAIGN ACTIVITIES
Adapted from the Alliance for Justice

The chart below offers some at-a-glance information about the rules for tax-exempt organizations this year. We attempted to simplify and condense a good deal of complex information: The intersection of election laws (federal and state) and tax-exempt organization laws has become so complex (and is changing so fast) that we strongly recommend that you get in-depth legal advice about how this information applies to your organization and your situation.

	501(c)(3)	501(c)(4)	527
Description	▨ Religious, charitable, scientific, or educational organization.	▨ Social welfare organization.	▨ Campaign committee, political party, or PAC.
Key Tax Rules	▨ Tax-exempt. ▨ Contributors may receive a tax deduction for contributions. ▨ No federal gift tax on contributions.	▨ Tax-exempt, but contributors do not receive a deduction. ▨ Donors may owe federal gift tax on contributions greater than $11,000. ▨ Organization taxed on investment income to the extent of electioneering expenditures.	▨ No tax on political contributions spent on permitted political activities. ▨ Net business and/or investment income is taxed at the highest corporate rate. ▨ No federal gift tax on contributions.
General Permitted Activities	▨ For public charities, charitable and educational activities, including public education and limited lobbying.	▨ May engage in any activity permitted a 501(c)(3), plus any activity that serves public purposes, such as unlimited lobbying and advocacy in the public interest.	▨ Candidate-related political activities. ▨ Non-candidate related political activities (may give rise to tax.)
Is Lobbying Allowed?	▨ For public charities: Yes, to a limited extent, subject to either 501(h) limits or to the requirement that lobbying not be "substantial." ▨ Private foundations: No lobbying allowed.	▨ Yes, lobbying may even be the exclusive activity of a 501(c)(4).	▨ Lobbying is not an exempt activity and may give rise to tax, unless done in support of candidate/electoral work.
Affiliation with 527 Allowed?	▨ No, but affiliated 501(c)(4) may have a 527.	▨ Yes.	▨ Not applicable.
Which Campaign Related Activities Are Allowed?	▨ Nonpartisan voter registration, voter education, and get-out-the vote efforts. Public education and candidate forums. Ballot initiatives, within lobbying limits. Candidate campaign intervention is strictly prohibited.	▨ Nonpartisan activities as permitted for 501(c)(3)s. May engage in candidate electioneering, as long as it is not the organization's primary activity.	▨ Unlimited partisan candidate electioneering activities.

	501(c)(3)	501(c)(4)	527
Is Express Advocacy Allowed?	▨ No; tax laws prohibit any campaign intervention, including express advocacy.	▨ Federal election laws prohibit express advocacy by corporations (including nonprofits) unless organization qualifies under the "MCFL" exemption.	▨ Permitted, provided organization registers any necessary disclosure reports under federal, state, or local election law.
What Issue Advocacy Activities Are Allowed?	▨ (c)(3) organizations may engage in a wide range of "issue advocacy" activities, including education and lobbying activities. Tax laws prohibit any issue advocacy that constitutes candidate electioneering.	▨ Neither election nor tax laws prohibit issue advocacy by (c)(4)s. ▨ But recent amendments to federal election law prohibit broadcast issue ads that feature a federal candidate and air within a certain period before an election, and those restrictions may be expanded. Tax law requires that any issue advocacy that constitutes candidate electioneering, taken together with any other candidate electioneering activities, may not be the primary activity of a (c)(4) in any year.	▨ Election laws do not limit issue advocacy of 527s; express advocacy communications are regulated by state and FEC rules. Under tax laws, 527s must be primarily involved in candidate-related electioneering, limiting the amount of non-electioneering issue advocacy they may do. They must also pay tax on non-electioneering expenditures. 527s that are federal political committees can air "electioneering communications" (broadcast ads featuring a federal candidate); the FEC may restrict electioneering communications by 527s that are not federal political committees.
What Disclosure of Donors is Required?	▨ The Form 990 requires some disclosure of donors to the IRS, but this information is not required to be publicly disclosed.	▨ Most (c)(4)s are not required to disclose their donors to the public. MCFL corporations making express advocacy independent expenditures must register and file regular, publicly available reports with the FEC, but these reports do not identify donors except for donors who give contributions specifically for express advocacy. State election laws may impose different disclosure requirements.	▨ If a PAC is a "federal political committee" (i.e., because it makes political contributions or expenditures for express advocacy relating to federal candidates), it must register and regularly file publicly available reports with the FEC. These reports must disclose the identity of contributors and the amount of their donations. Similar registration and reporting are required in many states for activities relating to state candidates. If a 527 does not file with the FEC or equivalent reports with a state election regulator, it is required to disclose its donors to the IRS on a form that is also available to the public.

	501(c)(3)	501(c)(4)	527
Message Considerations	All messages must be non-partisan, not crafted to help or hurt any candidates in an election. Issue advocacy messages that reflect a view on a legislator who is also a candidate are risky—consult legal counsel. Voter registration or GOTV messages should focus on the importance of voting for a broad range of nonpartisan reasons. Messages that constitute legislative lobbying (including lobbying on ballot measures) are limited, so stretch your lobbying limit by drafting messages that don't qualify as lobbying as defined in the IRS regulations, or use an IRS lobbying exception.	So long as other requirements are met (like maintaining a primarily social welfare purpose and keeping candidate electioneering secondary, or complying with FEC or state election laws on express advocacy communications, or Bipartisan Campaign Reform Act (BCRA) rules during the 30 days before a primary and 60 days before a general election), message content is unlimited; messages can be educational, lobbying, or candidate electioneering, including express advocacy.	All messages should be intended to help or hurt candidates for public office in their elections. If messages contain express advocacy, or name federal candidates during the 30 days before a primary and 60 days before a general election, FEC or state election rules may apply, and must be complied with.
Sample Message	"The people we elect this November will make important decisions about issues you care about—affordable housing, civil rights, and clean air, to name a few. Make your voice heard. Register and vote." "Elections may be the one time your elected officials have to listen to what you have to say—but only if you say it by voting." "In other countries—and in our country a hundred years ago—people died for the right to vote. All you have to do is register." "Affordable housing bill [name/number] will be voted on shortly. Make sure Senator Rye knows you want him to vote for it. Call Senator Rye's office now, at [phone number]." Note: (1) This last message is grass-roots lobbying, and would count toward lobbying limits. (2) If Senator Rye is a candidate for federal office, the legality of broadcasting this last message via TV, radio, or cable, during the 30 days before a primary and 60 days before a general election could be affected by rule changes being considered by the FEC; consult legal counsel for the latest information.	"Senator Pumpernickel has led the charge in undermining programs for affordable housing." Note: This message would be prohibited during the BCRA blackout period, 30 days before a primary and 60 days before the general election.	"Care about affordable housing? Then vote against Senator Pumpernickel." Note: This message assumes the 527 wishes to engage in express advocacy, and registers and reports to the FEC or any state elections agency with jurisdiction.
Sample Accountability Question	"Senator Rye, what is your position on affordable housing?"	"Senator Pumpernickel, why won't you support affordable housing?"	"Senator Pumpernickel, are you going to support affordable housing? If not, we must urge the community not to vote for you!"

AND NOW, A WORD FROM OUR LAWYERS

In the process of creating this publication, we learned a good deal about the activities that Section 501(c)(3) nonprofits can engage in during the election year. The Q& A that follows is drawn from questions we asked of our lawyers at Silk, Adler and Colvin, a San Francisco firm specializing in the law of tax-exempt nonprofit organizations.

Is it OK to ask candidates to take a pledge or make a campaign promise on a certain issue?

No. Asking a candidate to pledge to support a charity's position on an issue if elected could be treated as a prohibited attempt to influence the election, since the IRS assumes a charity would only seek such a pledge in order to publicize the candidate's response to voters so as to influence his or her chances for election.

While this is not a book that advocates for any identified candidate or party, we talk about "mobilizing progressives" and "out-organizing the right" to build power for grassroots communities. Is this OK?

It depends on the context, and specifically whether the activity is strictly about issues without any reference to the election or candidates, or whether the activity is election-related, like voter registration or GOTV. The IRS has expressed the view that labels like "liberal," "right-wing," or "progressive" can be coded impermissible references to candidates in the context of election-related activity. If a Section 501(c)(3) organization sends a message to recruit volunteers for a get-out-the-vote campaign for November 2004, for example, it would be risky to urge supporters

to participate in order to help the charity "mobilize progressives." In that context, the phrase "mobilize progressives" could imply that the Section 501(c)(3) organization is trying to influence the outcome of a candidate election by targeting voters who are likely to vote for certain candidates. But in a communication that urges supporters to gather signatures against a proposed environmental regulation or to support proposed tax legislation, a reference to "out organizing the right" suggests only a vigorous attempt to prevail on the policy issue, not a forbidden purpose to elect or defeat certain candidates.

While it is not a good idea for a 501(c)(3) to target progressive or pro-choice or pro-environmental voters, it is generally OK for a 501(c)(3) to help the democratic process to function better. Therefore, it is acceptable for a 501(c)(3) to target its voter registration or GOTV efforts to traditionally underrepresented or disenfranchised groups, like the poor or some racial minorities. Also, it is usually acceptable for a 501(c)(3) to passively make available to its ordinary constituency nonpartisan voter registration materials where this does not involve actively reaching outside its regular operations to target new voters.

Can we safely comment on past election outcomes?

Carefully. It's OK for a 501(c)(3) to be critical of things like low turnout generally, or disenfranchisement of African-American voters in Florida, for example, but expressing negative views about the 2000 election generally, or negative statements about the final outcomes (like Bush being president), should be avoided, since those kinds of statements could easily be seen as saying you'd like Bush to lose in 2004, which is of course inappropriate for a 501(c)(3).

Some nonprofits want to encourage grassroots leaders and members of their communities to run for elected public office. Can a Section 501(c)(3) organization get involved in this?

Encouraging members of grassroots community groups to become candidates and run for public office is very hard to do on a nonpartisan basis, and is generally inappropriate for a Section 501(c)(3) organization. It is, of course, appropriate to encourage leadership in disadvantaged communities, or teach leadership or organizing skills around issues or communities, but candidate recruiting and training should be avoided.

Can Section 501(c)(3) organizations do legislative scorecards that publicize incumbent voting records?

This depends on the timing, distribution, and format of the scorecard.

In one ruling, the IRS decided that it was permissible for a Section 501(c)(3) organization to publish a scorecard reporting the votes of all incumbent legislators on certain issues of interest to the organization, even though the scorecard indicated the organization's positions on those issues. The scorecard would be published in the organization's member newsletter rather than broadly distributed to the public. It would cover the records of all incumbents, and would not identify which legislators were candidates for reelection. The scorecard was distributed as soon as possible after the close of the legislative session—it was not timed to coincide with any electoral campaign—and it was not targeted to areas where elections were

taking place. Under these circumstances, the IRS found that the scorecard was a permissible educational activity, not prohibited electioneering. This ruling gives charities a safe example to follow of an appropriate legislative scorecard.

However, in another ruling, the IRS decided that a Section 501(c)(3) organization would violate the ban on participating in candidate campaigns if it widely distributed a legislative scorecard focusing on land conservation issues among the electorate during an election campaign. This was true even though the scorecard did not contain express statements of support for, or opposition to, any candidate. Because of this ruling, a charity cannot safely distribute a scorecard outside its usual audience of donors and members if the scorecard deals only with a limited range of issues.

If my 501(c)(3) organization is creating a legislative scorecard, can we distribute it beyond our own membership?

Generally speaking, it is risky to distribute a legislative scorecard on issues of interest to the 501(c)(3) beyond the usual membership or mailing list; the IRS may interpret this as an attempt to sway voters.

However, the IRS has issued one ruling deciding that it was permissible for a 501(c)(3) to distribute a legislative scorecard to the general public each year. In this case, the scorecard covered incumbent voting records on major legislation covering a wide range of subjects. The publication contained no editorial opinion, and neither its contents nor its structure implied approval or disapproval of any legislators or their voting records.

A scorecard that follows this model must avoid characterizing any particular legislative votes as "good" or "bad," and should cover a range of issues of interest to the general public and not just issues that relate to the organization's agenda. Of course, the scorecard must cover all members of the legislature and refrain from mentioning which legislators are candidates for reelection. If these guidelines are rigorously followed, a Section 501(c)(3) organization can safely distribute a legislative scorecard to the general public.

You've mentioned that Section 501(c)(3) groups must be careful of "wedge issues." Can you provide more context? For example, let's say a gay and lesbian rights organization has been looking at gay marriage as one of their core advocacy issues for the past several years, and that is an issue that seems likely to emerge as a big campaign issue in 2004. What advice would you provide?

A public communication that on its face advocates a position on an issue can be used as way to influence candidate elections. This is particularly true when the issue advocacy occurs during an election campaign and focuses on an issue on which the candidates differ. The IRS looks at all of the circumstances surrounding an issue communication to determine whether or not it should be considered an attempt to influence candidate elections. Some negative factors are:

- The communication identifies a candidate for public office

- The timing of the communication coincides with an electoral campaign

- The communication is targeted to a geographic area where an election is taking place

- The communication identifies a candidate's position on the policy issue it addresses

- The position of the candidate on the public policy issue has been raised as distinguishing the candidate from others in the campaign, either in the communication itself or other public communications

- The communication is not part of an ongoing series of substantially similar advocacy communications by the organization on the same issue

Positive factors include the absence of any of the negative factors listed above, and also include:

- The communication identifies specific legislation, or an event outside the control of the organization, that the organization hopes to influence

- The timing of the communication coincides with a specific event outside the control of the organization that the organization hopes to influence, such as a legislative vote

- The communication identifies the candidate solely as a government official who is in a position to act on the issue in connection with the specific event (such as a legislator who is eligible to vote on the legislation), or solely in the list of key or principal sponsors of the legislation that is the subject of the communication

When a Section 501(c)(3) organization wants to run an advertisement or send a mailing about a wedge issue that distinguishes the candidates during an election year, it should minimize the negative factors and maximize the positive ones in order to avoid any appearance that the communication is an attempt to influence the election.

If an organization wanted to run ads supporting gay marriage, for example, it would be wise to avoid identifying (explicitly or by implication) any candidates for office in the ads, or to identify candidates only for the purpose of naming sponsors of certain legislation the organization wished to oppose, or to identify candidates as officials with the power to issue marriage licenses to gay couples. It would also be wise for the organization to avoid targeting its ad to battleground states or scheduling the ad to run just before an election (unless the ad was focused on a legislative vote or hearing scheduled to occur shortly before Election Day.) Finally, it is less risky for the organization to run ads that are similar in audience, content, and timing to ads that it ran in previous years; it is more risky to launch a new campaign focusing on a wedge issue right before an election.

Can a Section 501(c)(3) organization use the excitement about campaign issues to register voters or get them to the polls?

The cautious rule for nonpartisan, explicitly election-related activities, like voter registration and get-out-the-vote campaigns, is that no issue advocacy message should be included, especially not advocacy about wedge issues that distinguish the candidates.

A nonpartisan voter registration or get-out-the-vote campaign can remind potential voters that elections will make a difference in issues they care about, as long as the messages remain neutral and do not favor some candidates over others. For example, a Section 501(c)(3) organization could use the following message, which does not signal a preference for one candidate over another:

"Who leads our country depends on you. Issues of war and peace, taxes and spending, jobs and the environment, and health care hang in the balance. Register now and vote."

Can Section 501(c)(3) organizations get involved in ballot measure campaigns when the ballot measure is a campaign issue in a candidate race?

Section 501(c)(3) organizations that are public charities under IRS rules (and not private foundations) can support or oppose ballot measures to promote public policies that advance their missions, but they cannot use ballot measures as a pretext to impact candidate elections. Thus, a 501(c)(3) could support a ballot measure in order to educate the public on an issue or to change the law, but not as a sneaky way to increase turnout of progressive voters or to frame the election with issues that favor progressive candidates. We understand that ballot measures are frequently used by political operatives to help or hurt candidates, and the IRS understands this, too; in fact, the IRS ruled in one case that supporting a ballot measure in order to influence a candidate race is indeed considered to be partisan electioneering. The IRS will consider all facts and circumstances to determine whether a nonprofit's ballot measure work was legitimate lobbying or prohibited candidate electioneering.

If a particular ballot measure becomes a campaign issue, or closely identified with one candidate or political party, or if a candidate or political party controls the committee promot-

ing or opposing a measure, Section 501(c)(3) organizations that want to get involved in supporting or opposing the measure for legitimate reasons will have to take extreme care in planning their activities to prevent any appearance of intervening in the candidate election, and should document their issue-based reasons for choosing to get involved.

Finally, totally independent of the candidate electioneering prohibition, remember that ballot measures are legislation, for purposes of the tax-law limits on charity lobbying. A public charity must decide whether its communications on a ballot measure are direct lobbying or qualify for some exception, must track its lobbying expenditures, and must monitor total lobbying expenditures to ensure they stay below legal limits; a private foundation cannot engage in or fund any communications that are considered lobbying communications under IRS rules.

Ballot measure activities are also regulated under campaign finance or election laws in many states and localities; a nonprofit planning to engage in ballot measure work should also make sure its activities are proper, or properly registered or reported, under those laws as needed.

What are the lessons you hope will remain fresh in the minds of community advocates?

Knowledge is power. Understanding the legal rules enables charities to greatly increase their public policy impact. While you may not be excited about learning arcane tax concepts, knowing the rules is crucial to playing the game. The policies you care about, and the people they affect, are worth the effort.

Silk, Adler and Colvin is a firm specializing in the law of nonprofit organizations. They represent grant-making institutions, schools, trade unions, and social service and advocacy organizations. The above Q&A is offered as a general overview, for informational purposes only. It is not intended to, and does not, constitute legal advice or a legal opinion. You should not act or rely upon any information that you obtain from this overview without first seeking the advice of an attorney regarding the facts of your specific situation.

Section III

FRAMING
A PROGRESSIVE
AGENDA

Before developing your strategies and tactics, you have to decide on the tale you will tell. Your challenge is to figure out how to craft communication so it taps into shared values, yokes problems and solutions, educates the media, policy makers, and the public, and wins allies and champions. In sum, you need to know how to frame.

Framing is the art and science of organizing information in a way that connects to what people already think, aligns with what they already know, and helps them see new ideas in a context that acknowledges and builds on their values. This section will help you figure out how to develop an effective frame.

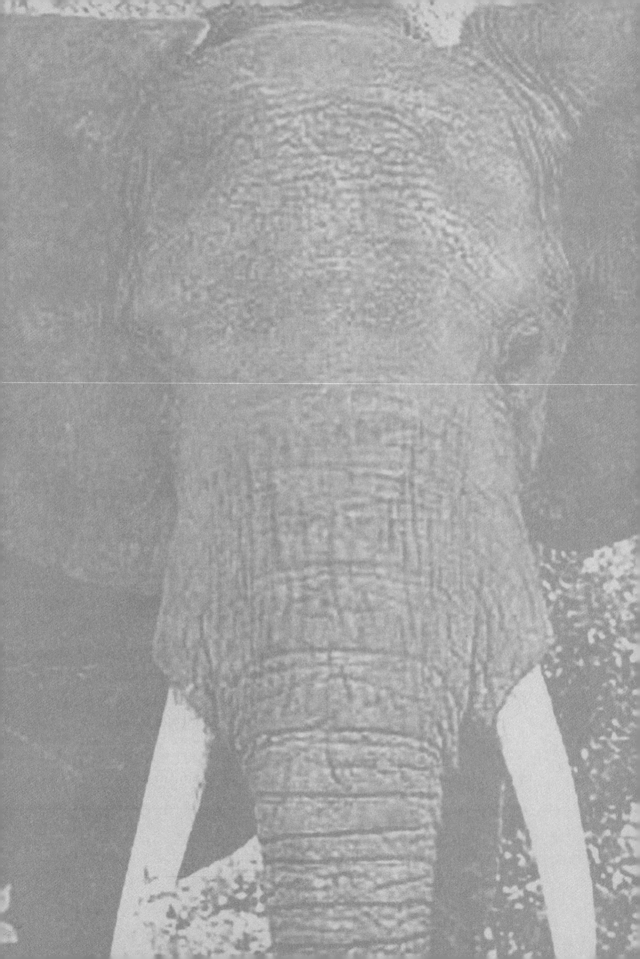

FRAMING A PROGRESSIVE AGENDA:
THE BASICS

By George Lakoff

Carry out the following directive: *Don't think of an elephant!*

It is, of course, a directive that can't be carried out—and that is the point. In order to purposefully *not* think of an elephant, you have to think of an elephant. There are four morals to this observation.

Moral 1: Every word evokes a frame. A frame is a conceptual structure used in thinking. The word *elephant* evokes a frame with an image of an elephant and certain knowledge: an elephant is a large animal (a mammal) with large floppy ears, a trunk that functions like both a nose and a hand, large stump-like legs, and so on.

Moral 2: Words defined within a frame evoke the frame. The word "trunk," as in the sentence *Sam picked up the peanut with his trunk,* evokes the elephant frame and suggests that "Sam" is the name of an elephant.

Moral 3: Negating a frame evokes the frame. The suggestion not to think of an elephant invokes the elephant.

Moral 4: Evoking a frame reinforces that frame. Every frame is realized in the brain by neural circuitry. Every time a neural circuit is activated, it is strengthened.

Conservatives Know About Framing

On the day that the current administration took office, the words "tax relief" started appearing in White House communiqués to the press and in official speeches and reports by conservatives. Let's look in detail at the framing evoked by this term.

The word *relief* evokes a frame in which there is a blameless *afflicted person* who we identify with and who has some *affliction*, some pain or harm that is imposed by some external *cause-of-pain*. *Relief* is the taking away of the pain or harm, and it is brought about by some *reliever-of-pain*.

The *relief* frame is an instance of a more general *rescue* scenario, in which there are a Hero (the *Reliever-of-pain*), a Victim (the *Afflicted*), a Crime *(the Affliction)*, A Villain (the *Cause-of-Affliction*), and a Rescue (the *Pain Relief*). The Hero is inherently good, the Villain is evil, and the Victim after the Rescue owes gratitude to the Hero.

The term *tax relief* evokes all of this and more. *Taxes*, in this phrase, are the affliction (the crime), proponents of taxes are the causes-of-affliction (the villains), the taxpayer is the afflicted victim, and the proponents of "tax relief" are the heroes who deserve the taxpayers' gratitude.

Every time the phrase *tax relief* is used and heard or read by millions of people, the more this view of taxation as an affliction and conservatives as heroes gets reinforced.

Once the "tax relief" frame caught on, the administration started using the slogan "Tax relief creates jobs." Looking at the relief frame, we see that afflictions and pain can be quantified, and there can be more or less relief. By the logic of framing (*not* the logic of economics!), if tax relief creates jobs, then more tax relief creates more jobs. That is just how the administration has been arguing for increasing tax cuts from $350 billion to $550 billion. The new frame incorporates the old Tax Relief frame into a new tax-relief-creates-jobs frame.

Now suppose that a Senator goes on one of those Fox News shows in which hosts with differing political views argue. The way these shows work is that the conservative host states an issue using a conservative framing of that issue. The conservative host says: "The administration has observed that more tax relief creates more jobs. You have voted against tax relief. Why?"

The Senator is caught. Any attempt to answer the question as asked simply reinforces both the tax relief frame and the tax-relief-creates-jobs frame. The question builds in a conservative worldview and false "facts." Even to deny that "tax relief creates jobs" accepts the tax relief frame and re-inforces the tax-relief-creates-jobs frame.

The only response is to reframe. But you can't do it in a sound bite unless an appropriate language has been built up in advance. With more time, one can bridge to another frame. But that frame has to be comprehensible in advance.

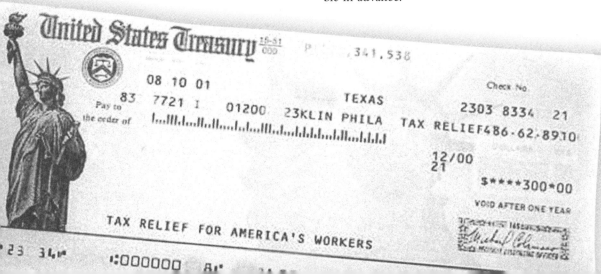

Jose, a retired farmworker, talks to a journalist before boarding the Immigrant Workers Freedom Ride in Los Angeles. Photo: Peter Holderness

Long-Term Reframing

Conservatives have worked for decades to establish the metaphors of taxation as a burden, an affliction, and an unfair punishment—all of which require "relief." They have also, over decades, built up the frame in which the wealthy create jobs according to that frame, giving the wealthy more wealth creates more jobs.

The power of these frames cannot be overcome immediately. Frame development takes time and work.

Reframing must express fundamental democratic values: empathy, responsibility, fairness, community, cooperation, doing our fair share. For example, successful opposition of tax cuts for the rich requires articulating over and over the moral basis for progressive taxation, in order to overcome the frame that wealthy people have amassed all their wealth by themselves. The truth is that the wealthy have received more from America than most Americans—not just wealth, but the infra-

structure that has allowed them to amass their wealth: banks, the Federal Reserve, the stock market, the Securities and Exchange Commission, the legal system, federally sponsored research, patents, tax supports, the military protection of foreign investments, and much, much more. American taxpayers support the infrastructure of wealth accumulation. It's only fair that those who benefit most should pay their fair share.

Reframing is telling the truth as we see it, telling it forcefully, straightforwardly, articulately, with moral conviction, and without hesitation. The language must fit the *conceptual reframing*—a reframing from the perspective of progressive morality. It's not just a matter of words, though the right words do help evoke a different frame: *paying their fair share, those who have received more, the infrastructure of wealth,* and so on.

Reframing requires a rewiring of the brain. That may take an investment of time, effort, and money.

Photo: Laura Saponara

There are two additional morals to consider:

Moral 5: The truth alone will not set you free. It has to be framed correctly.
Taxation is not an affliction. No tax cuts will create jobs. These are facts, but negating them as we just did just reinforces the tax relief frame. The right framing for the truth must be available and used for the truth to be heard.

Moral 6: If the truth doesn't fit the existing frame, the frame will stay in place and the truth will dissipate. It takes time and a lot of repetition for frames to become entrenched in the very synapses of people's brains. Moreover, they have to fit together in an overall coherent way for them to make sense.

Effective framing on a single issue must be both right and sensible. That is, it must fit into a system of frames (to be sensible) and must fit one's moral worldview (to be right).

Framing Versus Spin

Every word comes with one or more frames. Most frames are unconscious and have just developed naturally and haphazardly and have come into the public's mind through common use. But over the past 40 years, conservatives—using the intellectuals in their think tanks—have consciously and strategically crafted an overall conservative worldview, with a conservative moral framework. They have also invested heavily in language, of two varieties:

1. Language that fits their worldview, and hence evokes this worldview whenever used. "tax relief" is a good example.

2. Deceptive language that evokes frames conservatives don't really believe in but that the public approves of. Saying "Tax relief creates jobs" is an example—or referring to their environmental positions as being "clean," "healthy" and "safe."★

★ *The Rockridge Institute advises against the use of deceptive language and we will not engage in it. We believe that honest framing reinforces our values and is the most effective strategy overall.*

An Example: Naming Reflects Framing

There is a bill being introduced in the California legislature that will use the state's economy of scale to purchase health care relatively cheaply for workers whose employers don't provide it. Small businesses would contribute to a state fund and be able to purchase health insurance through the state at rates previously offered only to very large businesses. The state would be helping small business compete with large businesses in this way.

The question arose as to what to call it. Names suggested were "Play or Pay," "Healthy Workers," and so on. "Play or Pay" frames it as the unions strong-arming all employers into paying. "Healthy Workers" sounds like socialist realism. The issue is not settled, but I have proposed "Earned Care." The idea is simple: If you work, part of what you *earn* is affordable health care. It fits the belief system that health care is *earned* by people who work. Naming matters. The naming of legislation should reflect our values.

> Reframing is telling the truth as you see it, telling it forcefully, straightforwardly, articulately, with moral conviction, and without hesitation.

The Building Blocks of Policy-Making

Policies grow from morality. Values-based policy-making can be framed into five categories that define both a culture and a form of government as an alternative to the conservative vision. Those categories are:

Safety. Post-9/11, safety includes secure harbors, industrial facilities, and cities. It also includes safe neighborhoods (community policing) and schools (gun control); safe water, air, and food (a poison-free environment); safety on the job; and products that are safe to use. Safety implies health—health care for all, pre- and postnatal care for children, a focus on wellness and preventive care, and care for the elderly (Medicare, Social Security, and so on).

Freedom. Civil liberties must be protected and extended. Individual issues include gay rights, affirmative action, women's rights, and so on, but the moral issue is freedom. That includes freedom of motherhood—the freedom of a woman to decide whether, when, and with whom. It excludes state control of pregnancy. For there to be freedom, the media must be open to all. The airwaves must be kept public, and media monopolies (Murdoch, Clear Channel) broken up.

A Moral Economy. Prosperity is for everybody. Government makes investments, and those investments should reflect the overall public good. Corporate reform is necessary for a more ethical business environment. That means honest bookkeeping (for example, no free environmental dumping), no poisoning of people and the environment, and no exploitation of labor (living wages, safe workplaces, no intimidation). Corporations are chartered by and accountable to the public. Instead of maximizing only shareholder profits, corporations should be chartered to maximize stakeholder well-being, where shareholders, employees, communities, and the environment are all recognized and represented on corporate boards.

The bottom quarter of our workforce does absolutely essential work for the economy (caring for children, cleaning houses, producing agriculture, cooking, day laboring, and so on). Its members have earned the right to living wages and health care. But the economy is structured in such a way that they cannot be fairly compensated all the time by those who pay their salaries. The economy as a whole should decently compensate those who hold it up. Bill Clinton captured this idea when he declared that people who work hard and play by the rules shouldn't be poor. That validated an ethic of work, but also of community and nurturance.

Global Cooperation. The United States should function as a good world citizen, maximizing cooperation with other governments, not just seeking to maximize its wealth and military power. That means recognizing the same moral values internationally as domestically. An ethical foreign policy means the inclusion of issues previously left out: women's rights and education, children's rights, labor issues, poverty and hunger, the global environment and global health. Many of these concerns are now addressed through global civil society—international organizations dedicated to peacekeeping and nation building. As the Iraq debacle shows, this worldview is not naive; it is a more effective brand of realism.

The Future. For many Americans, our values center on our children's future—their education, their health, their prosperity, the environment they will inherit, and the global situation they will find themselves in. That is the moral perspective. The issues include everything from education (teacher salaries, class size, diversity) to the federal deficit (will they be burdened with our debt?) to global warming and the extinction of species (will there still be elephants and bananas?) to health (will their bodies be poisoned as a result of our policies, and will there be health care for them?). Securing that future is central to our values.

> **Reframing must express fundamental democratic values: empathy, responsibility, fairness, community, cooperation, doing our fair share.**

These are the central themes arching across politics, all deriving from values. That is an important point. A true vision must cut across the usual program and interest-group categories. What we need are strategic initiatives that change many things at once. For example, the New Apollo Program—an investment of hundreds of billions of dollars over ten years in alternative energy development (solar, wind, biomass, hydrogen)—is also a jobs program, a foreign-policy issue (freedom from dependence on Middle East oil), a health issue (clean air and water, many fewer poisons in our bodies), and an ecology issue (cleans up pollution, addresses global warming). Corporate reform is another such strategic initiative.

Excerpted, with permission, from "Framing A Democratic Agenda," by George Lakoff, The American Prospect, 9/24/03.

George Lakoff is Professor of Linguistics at the University of California at Berkeley and a Fellow at the Rockridge Institute. The Rockridge Institute is a group of distinguished scholars and researchers working to help achieve a just, democratic, environmentally sustainable, and humane society.

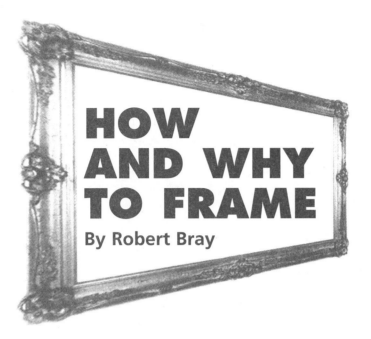

HOW AND WHY TO FRAME

By Robert Bray

Values-based framing is integral to advancing a proactive agenda. All too often community advocates construct the issue with facts and figures and statistics at the forefront. The arguments are reduced to pie charts and graphs. The framing model presented here will help you to break your issues into their most important and persuasive components, emphasize the values that drive your work, and appeal to hearts as well as minds. To illustrate a few points, I have included examples of successful framing strategies used by activists in recent campaigns for living wages.

We frame stories for two reasons:

▪ **To have maximum media impact.** The story framed most effectively will appeal to the media, help reporters and editors understand the significance and scope of the issue, cut through competition for news coverage, and score headlines. By framing the issue to include drama, controversy, reach, impact, human interest, and civic and economic consequences, you make the story more compelling and irresistible to the media. Aim your frame high. Frame so that your news has the potential to appear on Page 1A of your local newspaper, not be buried in the back pages.

▪ **To put the opposition on the defense and you on the offense.** Set the terms of the debate by framing the issue proactively. Whoever controls the frame controls the debate. Force your opposition to play framing "catch up" because you have articulated the issue in a way that serves your agenda.

HOW TO FRAME: A MODEL

Jobs, decent wages, "hard-working Americans," and economic recovery are key campaign talking points for all the candidates in an election year. The issue of living wage connects to these points because living wage campaigns in cities and towns around the country have helped lay the groundwork for a national dialogue on decent-paying jobs and economic justice. The fact that in many American households people are working two, three, or more jobs and still don't earn enough to live free of poverty cannot go unnoticed by the presidential candidates.

The living wage tactical framing model described here offers a template for how to frame a variety of issues for the election year.

Answer these specific questions to help determine your frame.

What is the issue "about?"

The issue can be "about" almost anything as long as it serves your agenda. Avoid framing the issue so narrowly that it is about something very small. For example, living wages can be framed simplistically as paying workers, say, $10.25 an hour. Or, it can be about something that affects the entire city or county, has dramatic and positive economic consequences, appeals to the core values of your community, and makes this issue one of the most important ones now being debated.

Who is affected by the issue?

Try to frame the story so that more people are affected by the issue, not simply the literal number of workers covered by the law.

Framing at Work: Winning Wages

"The genius of living wage campaigns has been to provide specific framings that highlight oft-hidden economic realities and fit progressive morality."
—George Lakoff

Living wage frames have incorporated numerous issues that cut across all movements, including poverty, workers' rights, economic justice, corporate responsibility, globalization, and more. Activists have succeeded in capturing interest and establishing broad impact with arguments such as "People who work should not live in poverty" and "Paying a living wage is good for our local economy and our families."

Here are four examples of frames you may want to adapt to your own work, as developed by George Lakoff and published in *Winning Wages: A Media Kit for Successful Living Wage Strategies,* by the SPIN Project and Tides Foundation:

The Community Benefit Frame

The more businesses pay living wages, then the more:

- The cost of community services will go down

- The economy will improve (more money spent)

- The self-respect of low-income residents will rise

- The general quality of life in the community will rise (less crime, drugs, homelessness)

- The moral level and reputation of the community will rise

- Property care and property values will rise

- Businesses will do better

Greater impact equals greater consequences and significance, which means more public interest and press attention. How many people will be affected? How wide is the *reach* of the issue? How deeply does the issue penetrate into your community's core concerns? Will your news only affect 29 people in your community, or does the issue have a much broader scope that will ultimately affect every person in your area?

Define the issue and players in your frame.

Whoever defines the debate controls it. Move *your* frame, not the frame of your opponents. The frame will determine who are the "good guys" and who are the "bad guys." Every drama needs a hero and villain. Frame so the opposition is on the defense and forced to counterframe, and you are on the offense, having claimed the public's understanding and the moral high ground.

Yes, it might appear simplistic to reduce the battle down to good and bad guys. However, by profiling the story and framing the players, you make moral and policy choices—and their consequences—clearer for the media and for the different sides of the debate, and, most importantly, for those who haven't taken a side yet.

Create hooks on which to hang your frame.

Reporters are always looking for news hooks, those aspects of the story that make it more timely and compelling. The more hooks contained in your story, the better the chances of the story scoring new headlines.

The Business Benefit Frame

If a business pays living wages, then:

- Morale will rise
- Turnover will fall
- Recruitment and training costs will fall
- Efficiency will rise

The Payment to Corporations Frame

If corporations are receiving payment from communities, then:

- Taxpayers will have less money to spend at home, as tax breaks and subsidies redistribute wealth from cities to corporations
- It's reasonable for the communities to get something in return

The Social Contract Frame

If we give corporations certain privileges, protections, and even payments, then:

- We expect certain ethical behavior in return: paying taxes, honest accounting, environmental responsibility, and paying employees a living wage

Frame with your values in mind.

We can appeal to the minds and hearts of constituents by framing with values in mind: values that uphold democratic principles and decency, that indicate what we believe in, what we stand for, and what kind of society we want to live in. Here are some of those values:

- Empathy
- Personal responsibility
- Justice
- Fairness
- Decency
- Sharing the fruits and benefits of our community
- Good business sense
- Work (working hard)
- Strong faith
- Strong families
- Opportunity
- Making a better life
- Dignity
- Civic participation
- Strong communities
- Public health
- Personal happiness
- Equal opportunity
- Public accountability
- Equanimity
- Character and contribution

To support and "transmit" your frame, consider what images, metaphors, and symbols communicate the frame.

What pictures embody your values and your frame? What media photo ops can you construct to symbolize the frame? During the debates over welfare reform in the 1990s, one of the most powerful and disturbing images that communicated the side of the welfare "reformers" were the shots of check-cashing/alcohol stores with African-American "welfare moms" waiting in line to cash their welfare checks.

Stage images that signify *your* frame. For example, living wage activists have staged events that showcase actual workers and their families, that expose the injustice of a poverty wage paid by employers who do not support the living wage law, and that indicate broad community support from clergy, business leaders, and working families.

Finally, target your reporters and frame the story in a way that's most pertinent to them.

How you frame for your local business reporter will be different from how you frame an issue for the lifestyle or political desks. How you would frame for *Oprah* is different from how you would frame for *The Wall Street Journal*. Customize your frame to fit the picture!

Think like a reporter. What will make this story of interest to them, and why? Why should they cover this story when there are dozens of others for them to cover? How can your frame and its hooks help reporters convince their editors to give the story bigger play?

Robert Bray is Founding Director and Senior Consultant at the SPIN Project, a nonprofit group of communications specialists who provide capacity-building to nonprofit public-interest organizations across the nation.

CASE STUDY
FRAME AND
BE HEARD

Case Studies from the Sierra Club
By Kim Haddow

The environmental movement is no stranger to framing challenges. Just remember the debate over spotted owls versus jobs, and you'll remember why the Sierra Club has been motivated to develop innovative framing strategies. Here are two case studies that illustrate their creative thinking.

Farms or Factories?

In April 2002, the Sierra Club filed suit against Tyson Foods and four of its 120 chicken houses in western Kentucky. At the core of the dispute was the "framing" of the nature of these facilities—whether they should be defined as "farms" or "factories." Riding this framing was the right to force confined animal feeding operations to follow environmental laws.

If defined as "factories," the ammonia emissions from manure in the poultry houses would be regarded as industrial pollution and regulated as in any other industry. If not, these "agricultural" emissions would continue to be exempt—as farms are—from environmental laws.

Clearly, the "solution" will be determined by which definition, or framing, prevails. If the operations are defined as "industrial," the solution is regulatory, societal and collectively applied. A "farm" frame promotes the perception of the problem as limited and the solution as individual (not collective) action; the responsibility rests with the farmer and not society.

Putting People Before Trees to Save the Forests

The Sierra Club has been engaged in a public debate over the Forest Service's wildfire management policies. Instead of continuing to let competing scientists squabble about the need for forest thinning and debate which diameter of trees should fall prey to the axe, the Sierra Club is working to "reframe" the debate by focusing on protecting communities, not just woods, from wildfires.

The Sierra Club has proposed the creation of "Community Protection Zones"—cleared areas that put 500 feet between the forest and businesses and communities now at the forest's edge. This may not sound like an earth-shattering idea, but it's altering the conversation about the Forest Service's priorities and budget. Arguing that protecting the health and safety of families and communities should come first puts the club in sync with most Americans, who value people over trees. If it succeeds, this framing could increase the protection of the community *and* the deep forest because logging big trees

We can do better!
We **can** protect
Iowa's air and water

www.iowa.sierraclub.org | (515) 277-8868 | iowa.chapter@sierraclub.org

Photo: Sierra Club

in the backcountry will take a back seat to clearing forest areas near development.

Framing the wildfire issue in terms of protecting people and their homes is a shortcut—a way to tap into core American values and put the conversation in terms people understand—home, family, community—while avoiding discussion of thinning four-inch-versus eight-inch-diameter trees, a conversation that few Americans are qualified or care to have. In addition, this framing offers a "solution"—a way out of the decades of zero-sum debate to find common ground, a plan of action based on shared values and priorities.

Staying Front and Center

Remember: When environmentalists are framed as "extremists," the goal is to distance environmental values from the values of Main Street America and to call into question the legitimacy of environmentalists' goals and tactics. Inside this frame, everything environmentalists do will be seen as shrill and absolutist. That's why stating shared values clearly, aligning ourselves with the concerns of neighbors and communities and with the universal need for clean and healthy air and water and for what John Muir called "special places to play in and pray in," are key to combating efforts to frame environmentalists as outside and apart from the concerns of most Americans.

CASE STUDY
ELECTION-YEAR OPPORTUNITIES FOR REFRAMING

By Amanda Cooper

In the fall of 2000, the Brennan Center for Justice filed a lawsuit to challenge Florida's permanent voting ban for people with past felony convictions. A "felon disenfranchisement" law hailing from 1868 deprives more than 750,000 Floridians of the right to vote—that's more than 6 percent of the voting-age population. A disproportionate number of those who have lost their vote are African-American. In fact, as many as one in four African-American men will be banned from voting for life in Florida if this law does not change.

Fortunately, two nonprofit organizations, The Sentencing Project and Human Rights Watch, had set the stage for the lawsuit with their landmark 1998 study, "Losing the Vote: The Impact of Felony Disenfranchisement Laws in the United States." With staggering statistics, including the revelation that nearly 4 million people nationwide had lost the right to vote, the study generated a good deal of press coverage.

Building on the attention generated by the study, the Brennan Center's communications strategy framed the lawsuit in terms of democracy and civic participation. Our frame tapped into core American values, including fairness, equality, responsibility, and patriotism.

Still, we had to manage our press outreach carefully, as former felons are not the most sympathetic plaintiff class—particularly in light of years of relentless media focus on crime. When we filed the lawsuit, we feared the media would focus on the nature of felony crimes, their impact on victims, and the recidivism rates of prisoners. To position our plaintiffs as the good guys in this story, we focused on the importance of voting rights in a healthy democracy, the sheer number of people whose voices are silenced, and the disproportionate impact on people of color. We also showed Floridians that their state was out of step, since people with past convictions can vote in more than 40 other states.

Our lead attorney on the case served as a federal prosecutor before coming to the Brennan Center. Her career path provided us with a strategic messenger to reinforce our frame. She started virtually every interview with reporters covering the case by saying, "As a former federal prosecutor, I can assure you that this case is not about crime, it's about democracy."

The day after the suit was filed, the *Miami Herald* ran a page-one story. The *Washington Post* also covered the filing. Between the September 22, 2000, filing date and voting day that November, the case generated 17 media stories, including a nationally syndicated column by Arianna Huffington, a *New York Times* story, a front-page story in the *National Law Journal,* and three editorials in Florida newspapers supporting restoring voting rights. Most of these stories carried our frame and focused on the intensely disproportionate racial impact of the law. This was excellent support for our litigation strategy, which required proving racial discrimination.

Then came November 7, 2000, the Election Day that wouldn't end. Voting rights in Florida became *the* story for the national audience. We capitalized on the limelight by reaching out to reporters who had expressed interest in the case and in voting rights, and by appealing to op-ed editors anxious to print pieces with a new angle on the election story. Here's our lead for an op-ed that ran in the *Chicago Tribune* on November 12, 2000:

> *As the entire country knows, a difference measured in hundreds of votes in Florida will determine the outcome of the presidential election, but few are aware that more than 525,000 Florida citizens were denied the right to vote in Tuesday's election.*

What Kind of Democracy Do We Want?

The question implied by our lawsuit is, "What kind of democracy do we want?" People were starting to think hard about this question in the wake of the 2000 presidential election. And most people believe that a good answer is: "a system that encourages participation and gathers input from the broadest possible range of people."

On December 19, 2003, the 11th Circuit Court of Appeals issued a decision that remands the case back to the district court for a full hearing on the facts and the merits. The issue, our frame, and our lawsuit continue to gain support and media coverage. In its illustrious wrap-up of "Ideas" for 2003, the *New York Times Magazine* called restoring voting rights for people with past convictions one of the hot issues of the year.

Amanda Cooper is the former Media Relations Manager of the Brennan Center for Justice at New York University School of Law. She now serves as Press Secretary of the labor union UNITE!

WINNING THE BATTLE OF THE STORY

By Ilyse Hogue and Patrick Reinsborough

"The universe is made of stories, not atoms."

—*Muriel Rukeyser*

Elections are the frame through which Americans are encouraged to direct our political attention span. Electoral politics has long been the realm of "politics as perception." This belief shapes each election cycle, as candidates jockey for moral authority over their adversaries and position their political agenda to co-opt the values of strategic constituencies. "Image politics" emphasizes personality over policy. Rhetoric trumps real equations for change and masks the misframing of important issues by all the candidates. At predictable intervals, electoral politics monopolizes the political imagination of mainstream American culture.

But by being creative, proactive, and strategic, you can make the election spectacle work for your community. You can ensure that when the candidates support community values, they also commit to take action on the issues. You can use election years to generate more airtime for the issues that matter and to reframe the issues in new and compelling contexts.

The Story of the Battle Versus The Battle of the Story

Creating a successful campaign requires analyzing and understanding the power of storytelling to structure information in a way that reaches and convinces people. Every campaign is inherently a conflict to control the framing of an issue between the status quo power holders and change agents. In this contest, you must make sure that you are not just telling the Story of the Battle, but truly fighting the Battle of the Story.

Too often, community advocates fall into the trap of believing that if they focus on the facts, then the issues will be self-evident. Then they proceed to bombard an information-saturated public with more facts and figures without explaining why. This is merely telling the Story of the Battle, which fails to frame an issue in a way that challenges the spectator role of the general public. For instance, when the news covers a demonstration as "protester versus police," the issue becomes framed as someone else's fight.

The Story of the Battle fails to challenge artificial dichotomies, such as jobs versus the environment or peace activists versus patriots. The Story of the Battle relies heavily on empirical examples that can be easily distorted and dismantled as exceptions rather than rules. Look at the current right-wing strategy of labeling every criticism "hate speech." Regardless of how preposterous it may be, it has forced many community groups to use their limited airtime defensively.

To succeed, frame your campaigns around the Battle of the Story. The Battle of the Story challenges prevailing assumptions and frames an issue. On February 15, 2003, the largest global demonstration in history took place as an estimated 15 million people took to the streets around the world to oppose the U.S. plans to illegally invade Iraq. While other demonstrations have fallen prey to quibbling over numbers or tactics, the *New York Times* front-page coverage of February 17 omitted the usual claims of skirmishes with police and instead proclaimed loudly that "there may still be two superpowers on the planet: the United States and world public opinion." In that single headline, the anti-war movement shifted from being a contentious minority to representing the global majority. The article focused on the inherent diversity of the crowd, and opened the process of mainstreaming dissent. Stories in major dailies around the world were written in a way that compelled readers to see anti-war efforts as large-scale common sense in action. For peace activists, this particular day marked a massive offensive in winning the Battle of the Story.

Shaping Your Story

To win the Battle of the Story, you need to understand how stories operate by breaking them down to key elements. There are many components to telling a good story—at smartMeme we use four main elements of storytelling to plan messages.

1. Conflict

Identify the conflict you want to highlight. Like any Hollywood blockbuster, social change movements are fraught with seat-gripping conflict and drama. You must be certain you are defining these stakes in your terms with your language.

2. Sympathetic Characters

Cast the sympathetic characters involved in your story. Pay close attention to who is receiving top billing as the messenger. Who are the heroes? Who are the villains? Frequently, the messenger is as compelling and powerful as the message, so choose carefully.

3. Show, Don't Tell

Nobody likes to be spoon-fed a worldview. People believe inherently in the right to make up their own minds. Become savvy about appealing to people's values. A question is often more powerful than a statement because it forces the audience to engage. Likewise, speaking in terms of values doesn't mean using the self-righteous political rhetoric of right and wrong; it means connecting your issues to the bigger concerns that shape people's lives.

4. Offer Vision

Your stories must articulate an alternative and more compelling vision. The visions articulated by community groups are too often steeped in the "sky's falling" metaphor. Problem is, the sky is still up there and people are tired of hearing about it. People don't want to think problems are insolvable. Society's fear of a vacuum often leads us to choose familiar evils over unknowns. It's up to you to provide the vision that makes the unknown alternatives real.

The good news is there are solutions that work—not only technical solutions like anti-pollution scrubbers in smokestacks, but policy solutions like getting money out of politics, and systemic solutions like building grassroots movements for real democracy. It's not enough just to criticize. People need to have tangible opportunities to engage not only their minds, but also their hearts and their hands. It's not enough to tear down the world; you must offer up what you would build in its place.

Truth to Power

Don't stop there, though! In order to win the Battle of the Story you must also understand and challenge the power holders' stories. The first step in retaking control of the narrative is to diligently compare your story with the one you are battling. There are critical lessons inherent in this exercise.

Frequently, when you stop to really look, you find that the power holders have framed the story using the same sympathetic characters that change agents use. Attacks on welfare are presented as benefiting working mothers. We are told corporate tax cuts are undertaken on behalf of the unemployed. Giant agribusiness firms use family farmers in their TV ads. The timber industry uses public concern about forest fires as an excuse to clear-cut our national forests. After the World Trade Organization talks collapsed in Seattle, the *Economist* magazine didn't put a sulking millionaire on the cover—it featured a starving child and claimed the protests would hurt the world's poor. Time and time again, power holders employ Orwellian logic by hijacking the real people who are sympathetic characters.

There is a big difference between appropriating someone's story and actually magnifying their voice. That's why community groups can ultimately win the Battle of the Story. Every day thousands of grassroots activists are fighting the Battle of the Story in their own communities as they work to build a more democratic, just, and ecologically sane society from the ground up. With all of your compelling stories, sensational conflicts, and infectious ideas, community advocates will ultimately outdo the multimillion-dollar PR campaigns and crack the media monopolies. Because the truth—at least when well told—is stronger than lies.

Ilyse Hogue and Patrick Reinsborough are cofounders of the smartMeme Strategy and Training Project. smartMeme works to combine grassroots movement-building with strategies to inject new ideas into the culture.

REFRAMING THE NATIONAL DIALOGUE:
LEARNING FROM THE RIGHT

By Frank Gilliam, Ph.D.

The evidence is pretty strong—the Right is "winning" on a number of social issues. Whether it's tax cuts, Medicare reform, school choice, or free-market health care, a radical transformation is occurring in the country's social policy agenda.

Over the past several decades, conservative values have grown more dominant in American life. While the stars may have aligned correctly for the conservatives, it is also true that the movement's members had a clear and simple message about their agenda. This is a necessary condition for any group or movement that wants to alter the country's social landscape. Let's look closely at the various framing strategies conservatives have employed.

> **"[W]hen a movement wishes to put forward a radically new set of ideas, it must engage in frame transformation: New values may have to be planted and nurtured, old meanings or understandings jettisoned, and erroneous beliefs or 'misframings' reframed."**
>
> **(See Sidney Tarrow, "Constructing Meanings through Action," in Frontiers in Social Movement Theory, Morris and Mueller, eds, Yale University Press, 1992: 188).**

The View from the Right: Frank Luntz on Language

One of the important engines for the Right's success in getting its message across has been its commitment to funding communications infrastructure and research capacity. Perhaps the clearest example of conservative thinking on the use of language comes from strategist Frank Luntz. In his monograph, "Language of the 21st Century," Luntz summarized the findings of more than 200 focus groups and provided ready-made applications for conservative politicians to use across a range of issues, from health care to the budget to affirmative action.

Conservative activists gathering signatures at a gun show. Photo: Scott Braley

Here is a paraphrase of Luntz's directives:

1. Principles are more important than politics or policy.
Americans aren't looking for an agenda; they are looking for principles and the politicians who exhibit them. In this vein, standing up for principles is more important than being loyal to a cause. For example, when it comes to health care issues, the Luntz report urges politicians to "use the values approach to communication." So while the policy agenda is completely consumer driven, the communications extoll the values of choice and security. As Luntz says, "It's about your doctor, your hospital, and your health care plan."

2. Embrace the moral agenda.
Americans believe we are facing a moral crisis. Luntz cites a broad body of data suggesting that people are uneasy about Americans' relationship to faith, family, and community. Luntz challenges conservatives not to shy away from discussing values. As he asserts,

"Talk about spirituality and faith in God, talk about 'family values', use words like 'values' and 'morality.'" For example, in a section on crime, Luntz counsels that policy reforms such as "jail, not bail," "protect victims' rights," and the "double time" clause should be cloaked in the language of individual responsibility, moral accountability, and fairness.

3. Focus on policy, stop talking politics.
When the subject becomes politics, change the subject to policy. For example, Luntz encourages his clients and colleagues to reject the impulse to get into a political debate about education reform. Instead, Luntz advises focusing on an education reform plan. A reform plan focuses on decentralizing federal authority and relinquishing power to the "towns and parents." It is a reaction to the failure of education bureaucrats to fashion an effective, results-oriented educational system (and speaks to an American public plenty aware of the failure of, primarily, public schools). Luntz tells conservatives to focus on

policies that support parental choice and involvement. Put more colloquially, sell programs on their merits without attacking the other side. Americans have had enough of partisan bickering.

4. Stop being defensive. Talk about the principles you are defending, not about strategic considerations. In other words, don't talk in public about "getting your message across," "end games," and "doing a better job of explaining."

WHAT'S IN A FRAME?

Frames are a composition of elements - visuals, values, stereotypes, and messengers - which, together, trigger an existing idea. They tell us what this communications is about. They signal what to pay attention to (and what not to), they allow us to fill in or infer missing information, and they set up a pattern of reasoning that influences decision outcomes. Framing, therefore, is a translation process between incoming information and the pictures in our heads. The nonprofit FrameWorks Institute describes a "frame" as the "labels the mind uses to find what it knows."

The FrameWorks Institute advances the nonprofit sector's communications capacity by identifying, translating, and modeling relevant scholarly research for framing the public discourse about social problems. Check us out at www.frameworksinstitute.org.

What Can Community Advocates Learn from Conservative Communications Techniques?

There are four clear lessons:

1. Build space

The Right has poured a great deal of resources into analyzing how communication interacts with people's existing belief systems. Foundation, business, and governmental elites have expended a great deal of energy supporting conservative thinkers to do and distribute their work. It's not only about providing money, it's about creating a space where thinkers and doers can work together.

2. Get clear on intentionality

The Right has been clear from the start that its members intended to revolutionize American life. As early as 1980, people such as conservative direct mail and marketing pioneer Richard Viguerie began to talk about using communications to retool the way Americans think about social life. No navel-gazing here.

3. Talk values

As the Luntz report makes clear, the battle is for the hearts and minds of the American public. The Right has understood that it's not about building the best widget; rather, it's about promoting a worldview that resonates with people's deeply held assumptions. Find ways to open the conversation; don't stop it cold with techno-speak.

4. Maintain discipline

It is painfully evident that effective communications strategies involve not only finding the right message but also having the discipline to stay on it. Any communications expert will say this is elemental. Exactly! Yet many community advocates do not practice this rigorous message discipline.

In all, we must renew our commitment to advocate for a values-driven social agenda. I hope this chapter motivates you to think about how we use communications to influence the national conversation about social issues.

Photo: David Bacon

Case Studies: **Successful Reframing by Racial Justice Advocates**

Successful Reframing by Racial Justice Advocates

How do community advocates refine, redirect, and remold communications, given the lessons on the preceding page? Here are two case studies from the field of racial justice that have put these lessons to work.

The University of Michigan Affirmative Action Decision
In June 2003, the U.S. Supreme Court affirmed the University of Michigan's use of race in the admissions process as a lawful means to obtain "the educational benefits that flow from a diverse student body." *Grutter versus Bollinger,* 539 U.S. 15 (2003).

The Michigan case had two effective framing elements. The first had to do with the *message*: "Affirmative action is the right thing to do because it benefits the broader society." At the FrameWorks Institute, we call this the Interdependence Frame. As Martin Luther

King Jr. said, "Whatever affects one directly, affects all indirectly."

The second had to do with the *messenger*. "Friend of the court" briefs filed in the Michigan court case by the business community and the military proved the power of what we call "unlikely messengers." In other words, people (or groups) with no obvious self-interest at stake testified before the public.

Taken together, these two frame components played a powerful role in the successful adjudication of the case at the Supreme Court. (Success may be only temporary, as the Right is now sponsoring legislation to overturn it.)

The Defeat of Prop 54 in California
Civil rights groups in California helped achieve an overwhelming defeat of Proposition 54, the so-called Racial Privacy Initiative, in 2003. Proposition 54 would

59

have banned California from collecting racial data in all but a few exempted areas. Opponents of Proposition 54 included then-Gubernatorial candidate Arnold Schwarzenegger, the civil rights community, labor unions, educators, and health care providers, advocates, and officials.

In this case, advocates made the decision to frame the debate as being "about" fairness but they did so through the "health" door. That is, they didn't think that simply pointing out that the proposition was racist would be the most effective way to highlight the questions of justice and fairness that the proposition raised. Thus, when people like former U.S. Surgeon General Dr. C. Everett Koop appeared in advertisements arguing that the measure wasn't fair because health care for innocent people would be affected (and they may even die!), the public was able to see the issue in terms of fairness or equity, using what we call the Equity Frame to come to a decision on how to vote. True enough, it will be back to square one if Prop. 54's chief advocate, Ward Connerly, and his associates succeed in reintroducing the measure with all medical data exempt. Meanwhile, Prop. 54 didn't pass, and in the process it raised the bar, and the stakes, for future debate.

Frank Gilliam is a Professor in the Department of Political Science at the University of California Los Angeles, where he also serves as Director of the Center for Communications and Community. A version of this article was originally published by the FrameWorks Institute, where Dr. Gilliam is a Collaborator and Fellow.

Photo: Danny Lyon/Magnum

MOVING YOUR
MESSAGE IN THE
ELECTIONS CYCLE

How are you going to fill the canvas inside your frame? How are you going to fill 2004 with the events, occasions, and media opportunities to advance your education and advocacy work? "Election-Cycle Benchmarks" in this section helps you identify the immovable dates on the calendar, such as filing deadlines and conventions, and advises on how you can use them to your advantage. It examines additional opportunities to reach out, educate, and persuade.

This section also explores the menu of message tools and strategies you can employ to accomplish your goals. Which tools—scorecards, reports, media tours, candidate forums, bird dogging—will get you the media and decision-maker attention you need to achieve your goals? This section will help you think it through and plan it out.

Photo: Martha Prescot, Mike Miller and Bob Moses registering voters in the Mississippi countryside, 1962.

ELECTION-CYCLE BENCHMARKS

By Kim Haddow

Timing is everything. Understanding the ebb and flow of the election cycle, knowing when the media are paying attention, when most of the public tunes in, when policy makers are most susceptible to pressure and eager for public praise will help you maximize media attention, increase public involvement and, given the new campaign finance reform rules, help keep you legal.

The goal is to ride, not buck these cycles—to use them to create and piggyback onto media and educational outreach opportunities for your issue. Mother's Day, for example isn't just a holiday, but a potential news hook to draw attention to the asthma epidemic or housing shortages. Understanding when the public and the media pay the most attention to campaigns can only increase the effectiveness of your communications.

THREE CALENDARS IN ONE

Think of the period from January to November, 2004 as three overlapping calendars: the election calendar, the political calendar, and the real-world calendar.

1. The Election Calendar

The election calendar is made up of the immoveable legal events that must occur within a cycle—and they all provide potential news hooks for your story:

Qualifying and filing for election. In most states, candidates are required to collect a minimum number of voter signatures that are turned into the secretary of state by a deadline; the secretary of state then certifies the names as legal, registered voters and declares the candidate eligible to file for election and appear on the ballot. Getting referenda on the ballot usually follows the same basic procedures and timelines—collecting names, submitting them for certification, qualifying them with elections officials. In addition, the wording of ballot measures must be approved by elections officials, who may require changes in the ballot language for legal reasons.

Conventions and other party gatherings. While they are thought of as massive political rallies, conventions have a role to play in winnowing the candidates by requiring that they meet a series of challenges—including receiving a vote of the majority—before they can become official nominees of a party.

Party meetings at county and state levels are opportunities to generate coverage and do public education. The meetings are largely staged, with lots of down time and little real news value, but the audience is important and full of influential people. As a 501(c)(3) nonprofit there are limits, but the following activities are possible, if carried out on a strictly nonpartisan basis:

- Setting up an information booth

- Holding a reception for politicians and the media or hosting a hospitality suite

- Handing out a clever lapel pin or other memorable material

- Staging a media event

- Flooding hotels where delegates are staying with materials

- Advertising in convention programs

Note that some of these activities may require equal treatment of meetings of all parties, so check in on the rules regarding the specifics of your plans.

Absentee ballots and early voting.

One of the biggest changes in campaigns is the growth of voting by early and absentee ballots. Almost half (22) of the states permit early voting by mail. In 2000, mail-in absentee ballots accounted for 25 percent of the votes cast in the general election. In Oregon, all statewide primaries and general elections are conducted exclusively by mail. Generally, absentee ballots can be requested within 30 to 60 days of the election. Absentee ballots provide another opportunity for a broader range of people to participate in the political process, and nonprofits should educate their members and constituencies that this option is available to them.

Primary and general election days.

All of your planning should work backward from these dates; use them to benchmark your nonpartisan voter registration targets and voter education efforts. In addition, because of new federal campaign finance reforms, certain advocacy groups must end

TV and radio advertising 30 days before the primary and 60 days before the general election. After that, grassroots and one-to-one communications will increase in importance. All federal election dates are listed on the Federal Elections Commission Web site at www.fec.gov.

- Know these dates: In most states, the secretary of state is responsible for overseeing elections. Most secretaries of state post their election calendar on their Web site. Voting registration is traditionally handled at the local level by the County Board of Registrars.

- Know the law: Every state is different. Some states, like Texas, allow early voting at set polling places. Some don't. Some states allow voters to register on Election Day; others don't. Familiarize yourself with your state's laws. For more information on your state, contact the secretary of state's office.

2. The Campaign Calendar

The campaign calendar is comprised of the traditional political activities that occur during an election year.

Legislative session. Incumbents use the election-year legislative session to secure their position and jockey for media coverage. This is the time—through bird-dogging and the like—to flush out an officeholder who's been coy about taking a position on your issue. You can also use the session to educate officeholders and the media if you invite them to tour your understaffed clinic, take a boat trip on the bay you're trying to protect, or expose them to life in a homeless shelter. During the session, release your report that outlines problems and offers policy and practical solutions. At the end of the session, release your nonpartisan scorecard. (Of course, you'll want to be very clear on laws governing lobbying activities for your organization.)

Photo: David Bacon

Announcement. Announcing one's candidacy was traditionally the event that made public a politician's ambition for higher office. But today, candidates campaign for months before announcing.

The announcement speech is important because it provides a synopsis of what issues the candidate will run on—and which issues will be avoided (which you'll want to prompt the media to ask about). Announcement speeches are usually accompanied by announcement tours, which provide a great and early opportunity to do some bird-dogging with signs that get the candidate's and media's attention. You should plan equal treatment of all candidates.

Retail political events. Tours of senior centers, visits to day-care facilities, and meet-and-greet sessions outside plant gates are all great opportunities for bird-dogging, showing off your own facility, planting a tough question for the candidate, or revealing a problem that needs remedy. Again, you must invite all candidates to participate. This can

also be the time when you call a candidate to accounts: "Today Senator Rye visited a day-care center, and soon she'll have an opportunity to vote on bill X that would ensure child care tax credits for working families. Call Senator Rye and make sure she knows you hope she'll support this issue."

Public campaign events. Debates and forums are great opportunities to elicit responses and get candidates on the record. As a 501(c)(3) organization you can sponsor or cosponsor your own debate or forum. You'll have to work with the candidates on a format that's acceptable to all candidates and the IRS, but regardless of the set-up, you should be able to ask your questions and have them answered. If you're attending a forum, contact sponsors ahead of time to be sure there will be an opportunity to have your questions heard.

Media events, news conferences, listening tours. You're allowed to attend news conferences and hand out your own nonpartisan materials, peacefully and respectfully, at the end. Candidates often conduct "listening tours" to learn what's on the minds of voters—be sure you have folks lined up who are willing to tell them. Your plans for these activities should include equal treatment of all candidates.

Advertising. Most newspapers run an "Ad Watch" column calling the candidates on inaccuracies or misleading statements in their paid political advertising. You can help reporters document the veracity of the ad by providing factual, nonpartisan information, or you can comment on it yourself.

Labor Day. One key fact about the political calendar you must take into account in your planning is that Labor Day is the day campaigns move into serious public mode, because most people are just starting to tune in to the election. Think of the pre-Labor Day campaign as the trial run or rehearsal for the candidates and your organization— you've had a chance to build a relationship with the candidates and the media, now it's time to think about the new audience that starts paying attention when the kids go back to school. Repeat yourself, say what you've been saying (your message) over and over— just when you're getting tired of it, people are starting to pay attention.

3. The Real-World Calendar

There's a telling scene in the film *The American President* about activists and advocates and their relationship to the real world. In it, one White House staffer asks two colleagues to take a break from work, explaining, "It's Christmas, after all." Her two coworkers look at each other dumbfounded: "Christmas?" "Yeah, didn't you get the memo?"

This may not be as big a stretch of the truth as it probably should be. And while this willingness to ignore the public calendar may be a sign of dedication and focus, it could also lead to poor communications planning. Schedule a public forum for Super Bowl Sunday, for example, and you'll find yourself in an empty hall and officially out of touch.

Mark your calendars with the major religious holidays and civic holidays, such as Earth Day, Mother's Day and Father's Day, Memorial Day, the Fourth of July, and Labor Day. Add major sporting events like the Super Bowl, March Madness, and the World Series. These are opportunities to join people in their community celebrations while making points in subtle ways. In my town's Fourth of July parade, for example, clean air activists march pushing hand lawn mowers. They make their point within the spirit of the occasion.

Pay special attention to the school calendar. When the kids are out of school, traffic volume changes and so do TV-viewing habits. (That's why the networks' rating sweeps are in September, November, February, and May— not in December or July.) When kids are on vacation, people aren't watching as much TV and they're not watching TV news with the same loyalty as when school is in and their routines are well established. The challenge is to go where the people go—that's why campaigns switch their buys to radio stations at the beach or the mountains in the summer. A news story that airs in mid-July isn't worth as much as one that airs mid-October.

The calendar is the basis of all communications planning—and that planning must be as attuned to the worlds of clients, constituents, and the media as it is sensitive to benchmarks of the election cycle.

Photo: David Bacon

NEXT STEPS

Map out the year.
Fill in the calendar with the dates from the three calendars described above. Add dates that are important to your organization or cause—the dates of your staff retreat, for example, or International Women's Day.

Figure out how to use the calendar to your advantage.
Can you piggyback onto a scheduled event? Can you exploit a lull in the established schedule when you could create an event or release material that captures the attention of candidates, media, and the public?

The following are media-generating tools and events you can create and schedule proactively. Each is explored in greater detail later in this chapter.

- Releasing reports that detail problems and solutions

- Releasing scorecards and report cards

- Conducting and releasing polling results and other research findings

- Bird-dogging

- Hosting candidate debates and forums

- Generating letters to the editor and op-ed pieces

- Rapid response to existing events in the election year news cycle

Be opportunistic and flexible.
A legislator may make a comment at a legislative hearing in the morning that you should applaud or rebut that afternoon. And remember, the news cycle works this way now: Feed your comment first to the paper's Web site, then to the radios, then TV, then the newspaper. By the time you call the newspaper to follow up, they may already have your quote from their Web site.

Be creative and have fun.

SCORECARDS, RANKINGS, AND REPORT CARDS

By Kim Haddow and Holly Minch

Scorecards, rankings, and report cards are three different products designed to educate the media and the public about lawmakers' voting records, to communicate your policy priorities through the votes you chart, and to hold incumbents accountable for the votes they cast.

These products give truth to the adage, "You can't tell the players without a program." These tools help the media and public tell the policy-making heroes from the zeros, using your definitions. The votes you choose to include on and leave off your scorecard or report card represent your policy agenda, define what your organization considers good and bad legislation or action, and publicly identify your supporters and opponents.

Legislative Scorecards

These can be great tools for 501(c)(3) organizations to educate the public on legislators' voting records on their issues. The beauty of scorecards is that they offer an objective and measured rating of lawmakers in a form that captures the attention of the media—which can't resist "top ten" lists or rankings of any kind, from Mr. Blackwell's Worst-Dressed list to *Rolling Stone*'s Top 500 Albums of All Time.

A legislative scorecard is a simple statement of fact, documenting how legislators voted on key issues during the session. Your scorecard should be published at the end of the legislative session—as soon as possible after the close of the session—and distributed to the usual members or mailing list of your organization. The publication should not be timed to coincide with any election, and the distribution should not be targeted towards areas where an election is occurring.

As you create your scorecard, you must document your issues across the board. If your issue is reproductive health, you can't score one legislator on funding for clinics and another on funding for abstinence-only sex education. You must score all the legislators on the same issues, and you must simply state whether a legislator voted yes or no on the bills you are choosing to score. You should provide a brief description of the bills, with information on why those specific pieces of legislation are important to your issue. You can state your organization's position on the bills in the scorecard, as a simple "support" or "oppose"—avoid hot rhetoric about the legislation discussed. Finally, document and verify your information. In creating the piece, use information readily available in the public record—sources like news articles, voting records, candidates' Web sites, etc.

See the example from the California Immigrant Welfare Collaborative on page 70.

Rankings and Report Cards

Of course, in a 501(c)(3) scorecard that focuses on voting records, there's no way to rank candidates—especially challengers who have no comparable voting record. That's why report cards can be valuable tools for 501(c)(4) organizations that want to give the public a sense of the candidates' relative positions on the issues.

But remember that even though report cards and rankings (like "The Ten Best Friends of Affordable Housing") can accommodate challengers by including actions they took while holding another office, or a public comment they made that expressed their position, these two tools suffer in comparison to scorecards. They're suspect because a statement isn't the same as a vote, and because ranking people by their statements rather than their votes inevitably involves some subjective decision-making—one person's "B" may be another's "C."

If you are a 501(c)(4) organization and decide to pursue a more subjective tool like a report card, be very clear about your scoring criteria. What constitutes a high mark for whatever grading scale you're using? It doesn't matter whether it's a green light, thumbs up, smiley face, yes/no, or A+, so long as it's clear. What did the candidate have to do in order to earn a smiley face instead of a frown? Note your methodology somewhere, with information about why the issues you chose are important, and what for you is the best position on the issue.

Also, choose your issues strategically. Select your top two or three priority issues, the ones you really want to draw attention to in the context of the election cycle. Which issues are likely to generate lots of media coverage for the election year? On your published piece, give all the candidates the same treatment—same size photos, consistent graphic design, etc. List the candidates in alphabetical order and present the information with no preferences. This is a statement of fact, documenting their positions on the issues.

See the example from Asian Pacific American Agenda Coalition on page 72.

Be the "Bible"

The goal should be to create a product that becomes the "bible" and makes you the go-to source on who is great and who ain't on your issue. Probably the best 501(c)(4) example of a scorecard that has transcended its use as a communications tool is the League of Conservation Voters' Annual Congressional Scorecard, which has become the measure of one congressman's "environmentalism" against another's. When candidates tout their LCV score in their campaign material and the media cite it in stories as shorthand for the candidates' environmental bona fides, there's no doubt this nonprofit's opinion has heft, both because the scorecard is defensible, and because the press and the public can trace the source of the scores. Legislative scorecards have the most credibility with the media because it's easy to see how the scores are assigned.

SAMPLE SCORECARD

Here's a sample legislative scorecard from the California Immigrant Welfare Collaborative. This is a great tool to educate people on the issues, and is appropriate to send to members and your organization's usual mailing list after the close of a legislative session.

VOTING RECORDS FOR CALIFORNIA STATE LEGISLATORS

Percentile Rankings

California State Senators

100% (0)
None

90-100% (12)
Alpert (D) – 92%
Bowen (D) – 92%
Burton (D) – 92%
Dunn (D) – 92%
Figueroa (D) – 92%
Kuehl (D) – 92%
Machado (D) – 92%
Ortiz (D) – 92%
Romero (D) – 92%
Soto (D) – 92%
Speier (D) – 92%
Torlakson (D) – 92%

80-90% (6)
Alarcón (D) – 83%
Chesbro (D) – 85%

80-90% (cont'd)
Murray (D) – 83%
O'Connell (D) – 83%
Perata (D) – 83%
Scott (D) – 83%

70-80% (4)
Escutia (D) – 77%
Karnette (D) – 75%
Polanco (D) – 77%
Sher (D) – 75%

50-70% (2)
Vasconcellos (D) – 69%
Vincent (D) – 54%

40-50% (3)
Costa (D) – 42%
McPherson (R) – 42%
Peace (D) – 42%

10-40% (1)
Margett (R) – 17%

0-10% (8)
Ackerman (R) – 8%
Battin (R) – 8%
Haynes (R) – 8%
McClintock (R) – 8%
Monteith (R) – 8%
Morrow (R) – 8%
Oller (R) – 8%
Poochigian (R) – 8%

0% (4)
Brulte (R)
Johannessen (R)
Johnson (R)
Knight (R)

KEY TO VOTING RECORDS

"Y" Voted in favor of the bill
"N" Voted against the bill
"NV" Not voting, absent, or excused
"–" No opportunity to vote on the bill

Notes:

- Votes recorded in the chart reflect the most recent vote. Endnotes reflect significant vote changes.
- Voting percentages reflect the number of times members' votes matched CIWC's positions. Bills on which members had no opportunity to vote (indicated by "-") were not used to calculate percentages.

California State Assembly Members

100% (0)
None

90-100% (36)
Alquist (D) – 93%
Aroner (D) – 93%
Chan (D) – 92%
Chavez (D) – 92%
Chu (D) – 92%
Cohn (D) – 92%
Corbett (D) – 93%
Correa (D) – 93%
Diaz (D) – 92%
Dutra (D) – 92%
Firebaugh (D) – 92%
Florez (D) – 92%
Frommer (D) – 92%
Goldberg (D) – 93%
Hertzberg (D) – 92%
Horton (D) – 92%
Jackson (D) – 92%
Keeley (D) – 93%
Kehoe (D) – 92%
Koretz (D) – 93%
Liu (D) – 92%
Longville (D) – 92%
Lowenthal (D) – 92%

(90-100% Cont'd.)
Migden (D) – 93%
Nation (D) – 92%
Negrete McLeod (D) – 92%
Pavley (D) – 93%
Reyes (D) – 92%
Salinas (D) – 92%
Shelley (D) – 92%
Simitian (D) – 93%
Steinberg (D) – 92%
Strom-Martin (D) – 92%
Thomson (D) – 93%
Washington (D) – 92%
Wesson (D) – 93%

80-90% (9)
Calderon (D) – 85%
Canciamilla (D) – 85%
Cardoza (D) – 85%
Cedillo (D) – 86%
Havice (D) – 85%
Matthews (D) – 85%
Nakano (D) – 85%
Wiggins (D) – 86%
Wright (D) – 86%

70-80% (5)
Cardenas (D) – 77%
Maldonado (R) – 71%
Oropeza (D) – 77%
Vargas (D) – 77%
Wayne (D) – 77%

60-70% (2)
Kelley (R) – 62%
Papan (D) – 64%

40-60% (1)
Pacheco, Rob (R) – 50%

30-40% (5)
Cogdill (R) – 38%
Daucher (R) – 36%
Maddox (R) – 31%
Richman (R) – 31%
Strickland (R) – 38%

20-30% (4)
Cox (R) – 23%
Dickerson (R) – 29%
Harman (R) – 23%
Leslie (R) – 23%

10-20% (8)
Briggs (R) – 15%
Campbell, Bill (R) – 15%
Campbell, John (R) – 15%
Leach (R) – 15%
Leonard (R) – 15%
Pescetti (R) – 15%
Wyman (R) – 15%
Zettel (R) – 14%

0-10% (8)
Aanestad (R) – 8%
Ashburn (R) – 7%
Bates (R) – 7%
Bogh (R) – 8%
Hollingsworth (R) – 8%
La Suer (R) – 7%
Mountjoy (R) – 8%
Wyland (R) – 8%

0% (2)
Pacheco, Rod (R)
Runner (R)

CALIFORNIA IMMIGRANT WELFARE COLLABORATIVE   *Voting Records for 2001-2002 Legislative Session*

SENATORS

BILL NUMBER	AB 60	AB 116	AB 540	AB 698	AB 788[1]	AB 800	AB 989	AB 2739	SB 59	SB 804	SB 987	SB 1156	SB 1818	AJR 57	VOTING RECORD
CIWC Position	Y	Y	Y	Y	Y	Y	Y	Y	Y	N	Y	Y	Y	Y	100%
Ackerman (R)	N	N	N	N[4]	-	N	-	N	N	N	N	N	N	N	8% (1 of 12)
Alpert (D)	Y	Y	Y	Y	-	Y	-	Y	Y	Y	Y	Y	Y	Y	92% (11 of 12)
Bowen (D)	Y	Y	Y	Y	-	Y	-	Y	Y	Y	Y	Y	Y	Y	92% (11 of 12)
Burton (D)	Y	Y	Y[3]	Y	-	Y	-	Y	Y	NV	Y[8]	Y	Y	Y	92% (11 of 12)
Costa (D)	NV[1]	Y	NV	Y	-	NV	-	Y	NV[7]	Y	Y	N	Y	NV	42% (5 of 12)
Escutia (D)	Y	Y	Y	NV[4]	-	Y	NV	Y	Y	Y	Y	Y	Y	Y	77% (10 of 13)
Haynes (R)	N	NV	N	N	-	N	N	N	N	N	N[8]	N	N	N	8% (1 of 13)
Johnson (R)	NV[1]	N[2]	N	NV[4]	-	N	-	N	NV[7]	NV	N[8]	NV	NV[9]	N	0% (0 of 12)
Knight (R)	N	NV[2]	N	N	-	NV	-	NV	NV[7]	NV	NV[8]	NV	NV[9]	NV	0% (0 of 12)
Machado (D)	Y	Y[2]	Y	Y	-	Y	-	Y	Y	Y	Y	Y	Y	Y	92% (11 of 12)
McClintock (R)	N[1]	N	N	N	-	N	-	N	N	N	N	N	N	N	8% (1 of 12)
Monteith (R)	NV[1]	N	NV	N	-	NV	-	N	N	N	N	N	N	N	8% (1 of 12)
Murray (D)	Y	Y	Y	NV[4]	-	Y	-	Y	Y[7]	Y	Y	Y	Y	Y	83% (10 of 12)
Oller (R)	N	N	N	N	-	N	-	N	N[7]	N	N	N	N[9]	N	8% (1 of 12)
Peace (D)	NV	NV	Y	Y	-	NV[6]	-	Y	NV[7]	Y	Y	Y	NV	NV	42% (5 of 12)
Polanco (D)	Y	NV	Y	Y	-	Y	Y	Y	Y	Y	NV	Y	Y	Y	77% (10 of 13)
Romero (D)	Y	Y	Y	Y	-	Y	Y	Y	Y	NV	Y	Y	Y	Y	92% (12 of 13)
Sher (D)	Y	Y	Y	Y[4]	-	Y	-	NV	Y	NV	Y	Y	Y	NV[10]	75% (9 of 12)
Speier (D)	Y	Y	Y	Y	-	Y	-	Y	Y	Y	Y	Y	Y[8]	Y	92% (11 of 12)
Vasconcellos (D)	Y	NV	Y	NV	-	Y	Y	Y	Y	Y	NV[8]	Y	Y	Y	69% (9 of 13)

[1] AB 788 was passed out of Assembly Appropriations but did not go before the full Assembly or the Senate.

CALIFORNIA IMMIGRANT WELFARE COLLABORATIVE   *Voting Records for 2001-2002 Legislative Session*

SAMPLE REPORT CARD

Here's a sample report card from Asian Pacific American Agenda Coalition, created in October 2002.

As we approach Election Day, the Asian Pacific American Agenda Coalition is pleased to present the results of its annual Candidate Report Card. This year's Report Card focuses on the race for Massachusetts governor.

The following table shows the results of APAAC's survey of candidates for governor of Massachusetts. A full copy of the survey, with each candidate's answers, is available online at www.apaac.org.

Please note that these scores are percentages. A perfect score would be 100%. APAAC wishes to thank all the candidates who invested time and effort in responding to the concerns of our community.

CANDIDATE	SCORE ON APAAC SURVEY
Shannon O'Brien (D)	71%
Mitt Romney (R)	declined to respond
Jill Stein (Green)	92 %

We are disappointed to report that Mitt Romney's campaign refused to answer the APAAC questionnaire. We provided Mr. Romney's staff with repeated opportunities to respond. We initially sent his campaign the questionnaire in April and resent it in September. At one point, Mr. Romney's staff explicitly committed to filling out the questionnaire, but later reneged. Mr. Romney's staff has stated that they refuse to answer the APAAC questionnaire because they believed the questions are "inflammatory." Mr. Romney's staff did agree to provide a statement to the Asian Pacific American community, which is available on our website. We feel the statement is an inadequate response to the concerns of our community.

HIGHLIGHTING YOUR ISSUE
WITH RESEARCH AND REPORTS

Adapted from *SPIN Works!*
available at www.spinproject.org

Releasing a report can be a good opportunity to raise the profile of your issue with the media. Reports and research are important components of a story's relevance in the election-year news cycle, because they provide the factual data and "testimony" to make the issue real and concrete. Reports not only provide information and facts; they also expose controversy, contextualize issues into broader political and social arenas, chart trends, and give voice to those affected.

Many community groups have commissioned research on their issue—or borrowed and customized existing data. One group released a broad, unbiased report called "Presidential Profiles" that documented the candidates' positions on children's issues—using information available in the public record. Another group, in lobbying for a ballot measure, released a "truth commission" report that exposed the lies of those who opposed the initiative. Whatever you report, it can be useful to garner media attention, move the story forward in the public mind, and educate voters, candidates, and elected officials about the issue. More important, reports will communicate your message and reinforce your frame.

There are specific ways to construct a report and release it to the media so that your issue is highlighted and your message is communicated most effectively. What follows are tips for making news with reports.

Constructing the Report

Think about how to construct the report to frame the issue and advance your message.

First and foremost, the report should be easy to read and factually accurate; all data should be corroborated and confirmed. Larger media outlets will often have fact-checkers peruse the report for statistical accuracy. If it doesn't measure up, it will be tossed.

Know the headline you want to generate with your report and work backward from there. The report should be constructed to support the "take away" message. Start with the title. Think about calling it something provocative and attention-getting. Use a tagline that frames the issue right from the beginning.

Beyond conforming to statistical and journalistic accuracy, the report will obviously reflect your frame. The goal of the report is to draw attention to the issue and frame it for maximum media and political impact so that it moves your messages and influences policy. Balance the statistical portion of the report—which can be dry and numerical — with aggressive, hard-hitting language that summarizes your findings and communicates your messages.

Your report should advocate and educate. Not only will community activists read it, but you want elected officials, policy makers, and reporters to use it, too. In fact, since reporters and officials are most likely your main target, prepare the report with this audience foremost in mind. The tone of the report must communicate academic integrity while maintaining a strong point of view.

Keep it short. Reporters don't have time to read long tomes.

Releasing the Report

Do not let the beautiful report you produce collect dust. You need a proactive media plan to communicate the report's messages. Following are key points to consider when planning for your media outreach.

- **Choose the appropriate strategy for making news.**
  Some reports may require a more low-key approach, such as briefing just one or two reporters you have cultivated on your issue (see below). Other reports deserve the full spin treatment: press events, rallies, photo ops—the works. For high-profile election-year issues, a press conference that presents the findings of the report coupled with a photo op rally would be a strong news-making package.

- **Determine the "scope" of the news.**
  Is your news national in scope with local tie-ins, or local in scope with national implications? Is it of interest to everyone in the state or the region? The scope of news, along with your budget and resources, will determine what kind of media effort to unleash.

Placing the Report with a Key Journalist

- Should you decide on the more subtle approach of placing the report with key journalists, you will most likely do so through a media briefing with the reporter or a collection of reporters and editors. Select reporters who are positioned to thread your issue into campaign coverage in their questions to candidates and other community leaders.

- Sometimes you can both "leak" the news to one key reporter *and* hold a media event to release it to everyone else. This is a commonly used strategy. Some news-making reports are given to a key reporter who does an advance story on it that comes out either the day of, or the day before, your media event. This can fuel coverage of the news by other reporters. This is called "pack journalism," when reporters rush together for a hot news story for fear of being left out. Of course, be aware that you cannot control exactly when, where, or how the story will come out with the original reporter, so there is some risk involved.

- A word about exclusives: Weigh your cost-benefit analysis carefully. If not chosen well, an exclusive can limit the amount of coverage you get. If you decide to give the report as an exclusive to one key reporter, be prepared for the positive and negative fallout. Positive: The exclusive results in the publication of a full article in advance that could trigger pack-journalism coverage of your media event to release the report. Negative: The exclusive causes other journalists to be irritated (or worse), if they know they were intentionally scooped on a good story. Do not give an exclusive to more than one media outlet. If you are going to provide an exclusive, make sure it is to the right media outlet in terms of size and reach of audience.

The Full-On Media Campaign

Do not release your report in some boring, fluorescent-lit meeting room, with serious officials reading numbers and statistics as reporters struggle to stay awake. *Stage* the news when you release the report, and give reporters a dramatic media *event* to punctuate it. If you decide on a full-fledged, multi-component media campaign to release your report, consider the following steps.

1. Produce a media kit that contains the report, your press release, supportive fact sheets, and other materials.

2. Stage an attention-getting media event that visualizes the news. This can be a press conference featuring key officials, the report author, along with personal "testifiers," as well as a photo op, such as a rally, protest, or other event. Give the media—in particular television—something to photograph.

3. Echo your message. Couple your media event with radio and television interviews, op-ed placements and other media tactics to keep the story alive and to broaden your exposure.

CASE STUDY

THE APOLLO ALLIANCE SOARS
WITH A WELL-EXECUTED REPORT RELEASE STRATEGY

By Holly Minch

The Apollo Alliance, a broad coalition of business, labor, environmental, farm, and civil rights groups, demonstrated exceptional savvy with the release of their "New Energy for America" report on the eve of the Iowa caucuses in January 2004. Named after JFK's 1961 program to put a man on the moon in less than a decade, the Apollo Alliance offers an ambitious plan to create more than 3 million new jobs in less than a decade by investing in the transition to new energy systems and modernizing America's energy infrastructure. This strategy will also rebuild cities, strengthen the economy, and free America from oil dependency.

The report the group released in January highlighted their plans for two key issues that already figure prominently on the election agenda: energy and the economy. The content of the report was both strategic and solid, firmly establishing and supporting their proposals on the issues.

Just as impressive as the ideas in the report was the release strategy the Alliance employed to ensure their ideas were heard:

- Their timing was impeccable. They chose the week before the Iowa caucus to release the report, ensuring their issue would be wrapped into the constant media coverage of the last-minute political jockeying.

- They made sure all the candidates' campaigns had a copy of the report, furthering their goal of educating the candidates on the issue.

- They took their report directly to the media with a press conference at the

Apollo Alliance members echo the message of their report with visibility events in Iowa. Photo: Apollo Alliance

National Press Club in Washington, D.C. Journalists just had to stroll across the hall from their offices to the briefing room to get the story.

- They provided one-stop shopping for political reporters by presenting their issues within the political and economic contexts of the election. Even their press release included a rundown of what key political players had to say about their ideas and a call for the winner of the 2004 presidential election to take leadership on America's energy economy.

- They engaged allies to help extend the reach of the story. The Sierra Club, the Steelworkers Union, and several key national elected officials posted the report on their Web sites and issued press releases in support of the plan, leveraging their networks and communications operations.

- They had a proactive strategy for keeping the story alive for several days, including placing the report with a sympathetic columnist at the *Washington Post*.

- They amplified the story by getting the candidates on record in response to their proposals—without extracting pledges from the candidates. The Alliance also let the candidates' views be known via their Web site, which included a sidebar on the report page with all the presidential candidates direct responses to the report.

- They used a small but smart field operation to keep candidates focused on the report in Iowa. A group of student organizers bird-dogged the candidates with positive messages and signs reading "Apollo: Clean Energy, Good Jobs." Because of the positive message, candidates welcomed the students at their events, with some even calling out to them from the stage. The consistent visibility created the impression that Apollo's ideas enjoyed broad public support.

The Apollo Alliance created a strategic—and successful—link between their research report, their field operation, and their public education efforts.

WE'VE GOTTA HAVE IT:
POLLS AND THE ELECTION-YEAR NEWS WINDOW

**Adapted from *SPIN Works!*
available at www.spinproject.org**

Many Americans are frustrated—and rightly so—with the media's obsession with horse-race campaign coverage and its emphasis on numbers above issues. But with a little creativity and a little money for research, you can turn this obsession into big news for your issue or organization. How? By using poll results to your advantage.

Polls are number-generating research that measures attitudes, beliefs, and attributes and shows the relationships among them. We hear about polls all the time. News organizations are constantly releasing results of public opinion polling on any number of topics. So, during an election year, when the media are constantly reporting poll results, why not provide them a poll on your issue?

While polls can be expensive, community and grassroots groups can benefit from the strategy. You can make a poll more affordable by piggybacking—buying a question or two on someone else's poll as they go into the field. Research firms often conduct omnibus polls, asking a number of questions on a whole range of issues. You may be able to find a place for your questions on one of these (see Resources, page 79).

Overall—whether you are making news with polls or not—polls can serve a larger purpose and help shape the messages and goals of an organization. Polls can help you increase your support base by giving you information that will help you present ideas and frame debates in ways that will generate the most support. Policy makers and candidates rely heavily on the results of polls, their own and others'. Your polling results can influence how they think on a variety of critical issues and what they know of your organization.

Making News with Your Poll

David Smith, former communications director for the Human Rights Campaign (HRC), a national political action committee for gays and lesbians, asserts that polls often help to bolster already existing news coverage or give a story new legs. Says Smith, "It's possible that you can add to a story by providing polling on any given topic that's relevant to that story."

He cites the following example: "Several years ago, when then-congressman Robert Dornan proposed a bill that would have kicked out all members of the military service who were HIV positive, the Human Rights Campaign did a spot poll and found that voters would oppose this measure. The results of that poll made it into several stories about the proposed amendment."

Resources

There are many polling consultants and organizations that carry out polls on any number of issues. The following are a few that have worked with nonprofit groups on issues with political resonance.

Global Strategy Group, Inc.
895 Broadway, 5th Floor
New York, NY 10003
212-260-8813
mail@globalstrategygroup.com
www.globalstrategygroup.com

Greenberg Quinlan Rosner Research, Inc.
10 G Street, NE Suite 400
Washington, DC 20002
202-478-8330
www.greenbergresearch.com

Lake, Snell, Perry & Associates
1726 M Street NW, Suite 500
Washington, DC 20036
202-776-9066
info@lspa.com
www.lakesnellperry.com

Peter Hart Research Associates
1724 Connecticut Avenue NW
Washington, DC 20009
202-234-5570
info@hartresearch.com
www.hartresearch.com

OFF-THE-SHELF POLLING DATA

Keeping up with public opinion can be tremendously helpful as you plan your organization's election-year activities. Many researchers make their information public, and they will certainly kick into high gear this election cycle. Here are some resources to help you keep up with the latest polls:

The Washington Post's online **On Politics** site offers the Data Directory as a guide to public opinion data published on the Internet by nonpartisan organizations: www.washingtonpost.com/ wp-srv/politics/polls/datadir.htm.

Pew Research Center for People and the Press is an independent opinion research group that studies attitudes toward the press, politics, and public policy issues: http://people-press.org.

The Roper Center for Public Opinion Research conducts custom research across organizations, builds and maintains a database of public opinion, and provides online databases for registered users and the general public: www.ropercenter.uconn.edu.

Pollingreport.com offers an independent, nonpartisan resource on trends in American public opinion.

OPINION EDITORIALS

**Adapted from *SPIN Works!*
available at www.spinproject.org**

In the crowded environment of election-year communications, one way of using the media to get your message directly to your audiences doesn't rely on reporters writing stories. You can write the story yourself with opinion editorials. Op-eds, as they are called, are often an underused device in the media toolkit, yet in many cases they represent the most-read pages of the newspaper. Op-eds allow you to move your messages in your own voice, in essay form, and in a way that captivates and galvanizes audiences.

Op-eds provide excellent opportunities to communicate human interest, facts, trends, and advocacy for your issue. They are particularly good at giving voice to real people affected by the issues that are at play in an election year.

TIPS FOR OPINION EDITORIALS

- Determine who is the best voice for the op-ed. Is it your executive director? Notable community leader? Campaign leaders? Community spokesperson personally affected by the issue? Clergy? Business representative? Think through your coalition partners, too—op-eds signed by unlikely or unexpected allies often have a much better chance of being placed than those penned by the usual suspects.

- If your spokespeople are writing in their personal capacity (not on paid time or using resources of your 501(c)(3) organization), they have a broader range of messages available to communicate. It should be made clear that the views expressed in the op-ed are personal and that any organizational affiliation is listed for identification purposes only.

- Make the op-ed timely. If a candidate mentions your issue on the campaign trail or begins to highlight your issue in stump speeches, take this as a convenient news hook. Don't write about something that's old news or already off the media radar screen.

- Write concisely: 500 to 800 words will usually do the trick. Check restrictions on op-ed length in your local paper. Use short sentences and short paragraphs— usually no more than three short sentences per paragraph.

- Make it personal, not academic. For op-eds with lots of numbers and statistics, boil the statistics down to the core, more important numbers, feature them first, and then sprinkle in human interest language that makes the numbers "real" in terms of how they affect people.

- Compose a captivating lead paragraph to catch readers' attention.

- Frame the issue within the first three paragraphs. Communicate your messages soon after framing the issue. One entire paragraph should contain just your messages. Repeat your messages at the end.

- Cite compelling examples or heart-tugging anecdotes to reinforce your position. For example, an op-ed on the importance of the economy in the 2004 elections could tell stories of workers toiling in two or more jobs just to make ends meet while they don't have time for their families.

- Irony and sarcasm are often lost on readers—and on editors. Don't waste your words trying to be clever. Be straightforward. Do use hard-hitting language.

- Pitch your essay to the op-ed editor or the editorial page editor. Call first to gauge their interest; then fax or e-mail the piece. Follow up to make sure it went through and ask if the paper is going to run it. Don't submit the op-ed to competing media. Go with your best shot first; if that doesn't work, try another media outlet—or rewrite it.

- Make certain the editor has your contact name and number.

- If you get the paper to run the op-ed on the day of your big media event, a big gold star to you!

Here's a fine example of a group using the elections as an opportunity to highlight their issue. The Liberty Hill Foundation has a very savvy—and successful—op-ed program, regularly submitting pieces to the Los Angeles Times, New York Times, *and other outlets. This piece ran in* La Opinión, *Los Angeles' Spanish language daily, on June 5, 2001, during the height of a hotly contested mayoral race in which progressive candidate Antonio Villaraigosa captured the hopes of the city's community activists and organizations. Villaraigosa lost the election, but the Liberty Hill Foundation achieved their dual goals of highlighting grassroots organizing and community issues, and reaching out to their Latino audience.*

Opinion
A Pattern of Leaping and Creeping

By Torie Osborn

A wealthy fundraiser for one of the losers in the April 10 primary shared a guilty secret with me the other day. When he got into the polling booth, he didn't vote for his man. "I had to be part of it," he said in a whisper. He voted for Villaraigosa.

All over Los Angeles, people are bursting out of their prescribed roles, transgressing their usual identities. Mayor Riordan is only the latest example. What's going on? Is it really just Villaraigosa's charisma?

Whatever his charms or leadership, no candidate for mayor can create a contagion. Crediting Villaraigosa mistakes symptom for source. The former Speaker's campaign may benefit from this local energy surge, but he is not generating it. What's happening in L.A. is bigger than candidate or campaign. It's bubbling up from below, buoying the campaign along with it.

Villaraigosa is riding the wave of a new social movement—an economic justice movement that's been years in the making. Los Angeles may not be the place historians look for the seeds of previous social movements, but L.A. is now ground zero for a movement that will shape Los Angeles for years to come. Eventually, it will reshape the rest of the country as well. Where better for it to get its start than in the city named the wealth and poverty capital of the country?

"New labor" usually gets the credit for birthing this movement. Local labor unions are adding workers faster than any place else in the country. L.A. witnessed a dramatic shift in public

Continues...

opinion when residents cheered striking janitors marching through the streets of Beverly Hills last year. The year before, in a historic vote, 74,000 home health care workers voted to unionize, the largest labor victory since 1945 in Detroit.

But new labor is only half the story. The other half—the unsung, unheralded half—is community organizing in low-income, mostly immigrant communities. In the last 10 years, Los Angeles has become home base to some of the most impressive and innovative community organizing in the country. Organizing that began in the 1980s in the wake of Central American and Asian immigration has achieved critical mass. It has combined with new forces in South L.A., rising out of the ashes of 1992.

In Pico-Union, Central American refugees are no longer preoccupied with survival. They're wielding power through civic participation and political clout. In El Monte, the discovery in 1995 of a slave-like sweatshop catalyzed organizing on behalf of workers in L.A.'s largest industry, 97 percent of whom are immigrants. In South L.A., Latino and African-American youth forged a coalition, united under the rallying cry "Bathrooms and Books," in a campaign to take back their schools.

Novel experiments in multiethnic community organizing have emerged in Los Angeles, coalitions unheard of anywhere else in the country. In 1993, Koreatown organizers began organizing Korean and Latino restaurant workers. L.A.'s Garment Worker Center, which opened this past January, advocates for garment industry employees in six languages—Thai, Laotian, Chinese, Vietnamese, Spanish, and English.

Unlike 10 years ago, vital community organizations are part of L.A.'s institutional landscape today. They are led by seasoned organizers, leaders who know not only the value but the necessity of organizing, coalition-building and keeping their eyes on the prize. These leaders and the citizens they've mobilized are the unsung heroes of this election, creating the excitement around the race.

Whoever wins June 5, this election has made clear that we are living in a new Los Angeles. Historian John D'Emilio says that the history of social progress is a pattern of "leaping and creeping"—how far you leap is dependent on how well you creep. For better than a decade, L.A. has crept along. Now, we're in mid-air.

Torie Osborn is executive director of Liberty Hill Foundation. She is a veteran social activist who has been championing human rights and economic justice for 35 years.

LETTERS TO THE EDITOR

Adapted from *SPIN Works!* available at www.spinproject.org

While often reactions to news already reported, Letters to the Editor can keep the story alive and the debate going. Journalism is one of the rare professions in which controversy is good. Reporters get extra points when their stories spark debate. A furious letters war on the Letters to the Editor page warms the hearts of reporters and delights editors. Among other things, it means people are reading the paper. But for you, it gives your news legs: The story keeps running long after the initial news was covered. Letters to the Editor are a great investment of time—with just 200 words, your message can appear in the most-read section of the paper.

Letters echo the message by appearing soon after a news story about the issue. They can refute mistruths of the opposition. They can help gauge the temperature of the populace. Policy makers and political candidates often use the letters page to keep track of the pulse of the community on the issues. The following tips will help you create letters that get printed—and read.

TIPS FOR LETTERS TO THE EDITOR

- Make them short and very concise. Letters should be no more than 150 to 200 words, or less than one typed, double-spaced page. The sentences and paragraphs should be even shorter than in op-eds.

- Make them timely. If the paper writes a story about what candidates are saying on your issue, respond with a letter!

- Make them personal. The best letters are those containing attention-getting information, often in the form of a (brief) personal story. Write no more than three or four short paragraphs: The first paragraph cites any previous coverage of a story: "In the January 2 issue of the *Daily Courier* you reported that Senator Pumpernickel unveiled a new health care plan...." The second paragraph introduces something personal and states your side of the argument: "As a person born and raised here in Our Town and who is currently raising two kids with no health benefits, I believe that...." The third paragraph moves the key messages—the same ones communicated in your press releases. "Health care should not be out of reach for working Americans like me." The fourth and final paragraph gives a "kicker" to the letter. "We need healthcare for our kids!"

- Sign all letters and provide a phone number. Most media will not run unsigned letters and will call to verify their authenticity. If confidentiality is an issue, you may request that your name be withheld from publication (check your local paper's policy on this).

- If your spokespeople are writing in their personal capacity (not on paid time or using resources of your 501(c)(3) organization) they have a broader range of messages available to communicate. It should be made clear that the views expressed in the letter are personal and that any organizational affiliation is listed for identification purposes only.

- Submit the letter via postal mail, fax, or e-mail, depending on your local media's preference. It is not necessary to contact the editor numerous times to check on the status of your piece. This annoys editors. One friendly heads-up call to be sure they received it is sufficient.

- Consider writing boiler-plate letters— standardized letters—that community folks in your "letters tree" can customize with their own personal information. Some people are letter factories and will submit one after another. Do not go overboard, but keep the letters coming.

- Remember that letters to the editor are one tool in your media kit. They are not the be-all and end-all of your media plan. Scoring a letter is valuable, but not as valuable as the front-page feature and the op-ed. Go for the grand slam: a feature, an op-ed, an editorial, *and* a slew of letters!

SAMPLE LETTER TO THE EDITOR IN SUPPORT OF THE RIGHT TO MARRY FOR SAME-SEX COUPLES

To the Editor:

With all the election-year rhetoric about American families and "healthy marriages," it seems that the presidential candidates have forgotten about millions of gay families and the millions of American kids whose mommies and daddies aren't allowed to marry.

The 2000 census showed huge growth since 1990 in the number of same-sex partners who have children: One out of three lesbian couples living in the same household are raising children, and one out of five gay males living in the same household are raising children. My family is one of the thousands described in these census statistics—my partner and I have been together fifteen years, and we're happily raising two children.

Lesbian and gay couples should have the freedom to marry. Only civil marriage can provide such vital protections and security to lesbian and gay families as the right to visit a hospitalized partner, custody and visitation rights for families, Social Security benefits to a surviving partner, and hundreds of other legal protections and responsibilities. It's only fair.

My family—and our two kids—are among those who are denied the rights that so many other American families enjoy. If the politicians are so eager to encourage healthy marriages, they should let us get married now.

Signed,

Name, title
Organization
City, state, date

STAGING MEDIA EVENTS:
GRAB ATTENTION FOR YOUR ISSUE

**Adapted from *SPIN Works!*
available at www.spinproject.org**

There are press conferences—and then there are media events. In our experience, reporters prefer the latter—and the difference is more than simple semantics.

Press conferences are typically characterized by highly controlled, formalized settings featuring official speakers delivering scripted comments, with a Q&A session following, all usually held indoors in an office-like space or briefing room. Press conferences are often called to respond to some news development, or to make news, such as releasing a report or making an announcement.

The most media-savvy organizations, however, create media events that transmit their message and capture the public's attention. Media events usually feature more spontaneity and contain elements of staging, drama, color, action, and surprise. While press conferences can present a visual image, media events usually feature more photo opportunities, making them more attractive to television. What to hold—a press conference or full-blown media event—depends on the nature of your news and the appropriate venue for it.

Media events are, well, *events*. They are *staged*. They feature groups of people doing something visually interesting that symbolizes your issue and evokes your message. They're often held in unusual or outdoor settings, and present unlikely speakers and perhaps a rally, vigil, protest, or street theater action that drives home your messages. The challenge is to find a way to dramatize and visualize your news to make it more interesting and appealing, in particular to television. Media events in general are more visual, spontaneous, and dramatic, but it's harder to manage the many elements and it's more difficult to control the message.

Whatever event you decide to do, if it's exciting, visually engaging, and newsworthy, you'll raise your chances of attracting reporters.

In his book *Making the News, A Guide for Nonprofits and Activists* (Westview Press, 2003), media activist Jason Salzman writes: "Successful media events are, above all else, entertaining. That doesn't mean amusing.... They are engaging, and that is the key synonym for entertainment in the media."

Staging Media Events

Keep the following tips in mind when planning media events.

Hold them only when you have news.

Reporters dread news events in which no news is made. Don't waste reporters' time with nonevents, or events designed simply to promote your name. Actually make news (new announcement, new report released, protest staged, etc.) at your event.

Decide if you need a media event.

Perhaps you don't need a full-blown media event to make news. Depending on your story, a well-placed phone call to pitch your story to a reporter, resulting in a feature article, may suffice. Or place an opinion editorial. Media events are labor intensive and costly, so conduct them sparingly. Sponsor too many events and reporters will begin to be skeptical of your intentions.

Determine the target audience for your news.

The audience for your news will determine what kind of event you stage and what media are invited. That means that where you stage the event, who speaks, what the banners look like, and numerous other details will be influenced by your target audience. For example, if you want to motivate young people in your community to vote, events promoting youth-related messages will look and sound very different from other kinds of events. You might stage your event at a location where young people congregate, and underscore the visual style with youth-culture graphics. Events like these should also be designed to attract media that serve young people, like radio, alternatively newsweeklies, zines, bloggers, etc.

Aim for a news day.

Schedule your event with the best timing in mind. Mondays aren't so good because you can have trouble reaching key reporters right before the event. Fridays aren't so good either, because the news may come out in Saturday's media—the least-read issue of the newspaper and the day people are relaxing or otherwise distracted.

Know what's a good time for media events.

Late morning is a good time for a press conference; lunch hour is best if you are trying to attract participants to a rally; and midweek is ideal in an otherwise slow news week. Of course, you can never really predict slow news days, and the reality of your organizing may dictate other times. Don't stage your events late in the afternoon or evening, when many reporters are on deadline. In addition, the Internet has speeded up the dissemination of fast-breaking news, and radio news can broadcast live almost any time of the day. Still, it pays to be aware of news "windows," times to maximize coverage. If you must stage a rally after work, for example, do it when the evening television news is on so the stations can send cameras for live coverage. If your event is on the weekend, make sure that key reporters who normally work during the week, as well as the weekend crew, know about the event.

Avoid being bumped.

Check for competing events. Beware of scheduling your news event on days when other major news will be made. For example, if the pope or the president is coming to your town, do not pick that day to make news unless it's related to their visits (in which case, do everything you can to make news). Same goes for days when major local events will dominate coverage, such as big civic parades or sporting spectacles. Your news event most likely will be bumped off the pages and airwaves in the competition for reporters' time. Check community contacts and calendars for what else is happening that day. Call around to other groups to see if they have anything scheduled.

Photo: Eric Wagner/Basetree.com

Dressed in bright pink cellophane, activists protest the absence of public scrutiny or Congressional oversight in the awarding of "reconstruction" contracts in Iraq. Their sign says, "What's in the Bechtel Contract? Transparency Now!"

Keep the event short.

A good media event lasts about 30 to 45 minutes. Beyond that, you'll begin to lose reporters. Major rallies, of course, may go on longer, but reporters will get their stories soon after the first few speakers and then head back to the newsroom to write them up.

Ger your message out at rallies and marches.

If your event is a major, all-day rally, march, or similar gathering, stack the key "message deliverers" toward the beginning of the event and instruct them to move the message from the stage. In fact, the very first speaker—besides being the welcoming host—should communicate the key messages at the outset, when media attention is highest. After the first few speakers, reporters tend to drift away to interview other people. The rest of the speaker line-up may or may not be heard by reporters, but at least the messages were communicated at the beginning.

Location. Location. Location.

Make the location appropriate to the issue. The backdrop should symbolize and frame the news, not distract from it. Make your event convenient to reporters, yet dynamic and appropriate in terms of backdrop. Do not make a pack of reporters travel hundreds or even dozens of miles to get the story. Bring the story to them if you have to. The further away from their newsrooms, the more reluctant they will be to cover it unless the event is earth-shattering in importance.

Keep it clean.

For 501(c)(3) funded, nonpartisan events, keep a written record that speakers were briefed on restrictions to what they can and can't communicate. This would include a briefing memo and signed agreement to abide by the rules. If candidates are in attendance, don't allow them to turn your event into a campaign event.

Check reporters in and rope off media areas.

Have reporters sign in at a check-in table at both press conferences and media events. Hand them press kits and schmooze them. Some press conferences offer reporters coffee or other refreshments. Don't offer anything lavish. For big, outdoor rally-type media events, inform reporters in an advance media advisory of the location of the press area—typically near the stage or the command center. Hang a big sign nearby that says "MEDIA." At big events, section off a designated media area (affectionately called a bullpen), where reporters can conduct interviews, rendezvous with sources, and generally hang out. The media area is a good place to have water and other refreshments and a cell phone. Control access to this area. Run your featured speakers through this area for media "availabilities" and one-on-one interviews.

Practice your event.

For press conferences, consider a "dress rehearsal" the day before with your speakers. Use it to fire questions that reporters may ask at the speakers and to test audio-visual equipment you may be using.

Spin and schmooze reporters.

Your media event is your time to shine, so greet each reporter personally, make sure they have statements and press kits, give them your business card or contact number, ensure they are comfortable and taken care

SPOKESFOLKS

Your spokespeople can make or break your media event, so be sure to plan your speakers' line-up carefully and prepare all your spokespeople in advance of the event.

Don't have more than three or four key speakers at media events. The first speaker frames the event, welcomes, hosts, introduces other speakers, and communicates the key messages. Other speakers echo the message and add depth. Keep it to five minutes maximum for each speaker. If you have the line-up set, publicize it to reporters in a media advisory. Hand out a list of speakers with short bios for each.

Here are typical speakers to include in a media event line-up:

- An executive director or other key staff person, board member, or designated spokesperson of your organization

- One or two people representing the personal human interest of your issue—moms, dads, kids, neighbors, and community members who are affected by policies and politics; these are often the best spokespeople on the issues

- A public official, celebrity, local politician, or ally

- An "expert," such as the author of the report you are releasing or the lawyer in charge of a case or a teacher, doctor, or scientist who can speak to your issue, as appropriate

Try for diversity in terms of speakers at your press conference or media event. Strive for a rich representation, including people of color, age, and gender diversity, as well as "types" of people (officials and regular folk). The idea of conducting a press conference that features a line-up of five white, straight men is unlikely to represent the audience you need to reach. Speaking at an official news event is an honor and carries with it community importance and personal significance. Use your position as a media activist to ensure that those rarely represented in the media are, in fact, featured at your media events.

Think about your friends. Allies and experts add value to your news events, but obviously they can't all be speakers or you'll be there all day (and reporters will leave). Feature these VIPs arrayed behind the podium in a row of distinguished experts. Introduce them and offer them for interviews and statements after the press conference. Include their statements in your press kit.

of, be a resource for them in terms of securing interviews and other information, and keep spinning the message to them. "Did you hear so-and-so speak?" one media activist could be heard asking a reporter. "I thought her point about such-and-such was so important because…."

Do your follow-up.

After the event or press conference is not the time to relax, even though you may be exhausted. Keep the adrenaline running for a few more hours. First, check the reporter sign-in list to see who showed up and who didn't. Call the no-shows and offer to courier over a press kit and pitch the story again. Key reporters who did show often appreciate a follow-up call to them back at the office so they can fill in any information they still need. Don't abandon your office or cellular phone. Stay close to a phone while reporters are writing the story on deadline—they may need an extra quote or quick fact-check.

CHECKLIST FOR NEWS EVENTS

Before the event:

- ☐ News defined.
- ☐ Audience targeted.
- ☐ Messages honed (talking points scripted).
- ☐ Location, time, and date scheduled.
- ☐ Room confirmed for press conference. Space confirmed for media event.
- ☐ Calendar checked for conflicts.
- ☐ Speakers identified and confirmed.
- ☐ Media advisory drafted and sent to reporters.
- ☐ Deliverables produced (press kit, reports, videos, etc.).
- ☐ Logistics team in place for media event (security, crew, volunteers, etc.).
- ☐ Decorations produced (banners, posters, podium logo, charts, etc.).
- ☐ Pitch calls to reporters made.
- ☐ Dress rehearsal scheduled for speakers at press conference/media event.
- ☐ AV equipment secured for space.
- ☐ Refreshments confirmed (if ordered).

At the press conference or media event:

- ☐ Bullpen media area roped off.
- ☐ Press kits stuffed and ready to be handed out. Signage put up.
- ☐ Test your AV, cue tape if you have one.
- ☐ Media check-in sheet put out. Someone assigned to staff the check-in desk at all times.
- ☐ Speakers show up.
- ☐ Props and decorations in place.
- ☐ Reporters greeted and checked in as they arrive.
- ☐ First speaker starts on time (within five minutes of scheduled time).
- ☐ Other speakers talk on time.
- ☐ Q&A period starts.
- ☐ Follow-up spin after Q&A.
- ☐ Follow-up work completed (no-shows contacted).

CASE STUDY

LEMONADE STAND

By Holly Minch

Here's an example of a group that took their event—and their issue—straight to the media with a creative, fun, and attention-grabbing media event!

During the 1999 Iowa caucuses, the Iowa Citizen Action Network (ICAN) was looking for a novel way to draw attention to their concerns about campaign finance. They struck gold when they decided to run their own candidate for president. They even helped her host her first fundraiser—a lemonade stand.

You see, their candidate was only four years old. Little Alexandra Cook figured that if she wants to run for president when she's old enough (in 2032), she'll need more than $100 million to finance her campaign, so she'd better start fundraising right away.

The group set up Alexandra's lemonade stand in front of the grounds where the straw poll festivities where held—and therefore under the nose of many of the journalists in town to cover the caucuses. ICAN launched Alexandra's candidacy,

complete with stickers, signs, and palm cards—all the trappings of a presidential campaign kick-off. On Straw Poll Sunday, Alexandra shook hands, posed for the media, and handed out campaign literature. But ICAN did have to cut the event short when Alexandra's campaign manager mom reminded reporters that their press conference was cutting into her daughter's nap time.

The group further amplified the reach of their event by putting Alexandra in the *New York Times*. The Web site TomPaine.com, which regularly publishes "op-ads" in the *Times* to highlight important issues from a public interest perspective, created an op-ad featuring Alexandra's story to drive home the group's demands for campaign finance reform.

With a little creative thinking, even child's play can make the news and educate people about your issue.

CANDIDATE FORUMS

Adapted from material created by the Western Progressive Leadership Network, a program of the Western States Center, with special thanks to consultants Thalia Zepatos, Liz Kaufman, and Holly Pruett

At the height of the election-year news cycle, candidate forums provide a chance for candidates to present their views and qualifications to voters and attempt to win support. They are also great opportunities for you to educate candidates on your priorities, raise the profile of your issue in debates among candidates, and inject your issues into the media coverage of the race. A candidate forum can offer your organization and constituency other benefits as well:

- Political education of members and the community
- Increased motivation to vote
- Political recognition of members and the community
- Relationship-building with elected officials
- Opportunity for media coverage of your issue

A candidate forum can be sponsored by a range of organizations, from the League of Women Voters to a community organization serving Latinos, gays and lesbians, workers—even yours!

The important thing is to keep it neutral. If you are a 501(c)(3) organization, you may conduct nonpartisan voter education activities, but you're strictly prohibited from taking a position in a candidate race. A 501(c)(3) candidate forum must cover a broad range of issues. 501(c)(4) organizations can engage in partisan activities (within limits); however,

doing so at a candidate forum, which is meant to air various points of view, can backfire.

Your questions can force the candidates to show themselves as either supportive or opposed to your goals; but as a sponsor, your group should not take sides or show its support for one candidate over another at the forum. Biased or loaded questions are not permissible for a 501(c)(3) organization. In other words, let the candidates speak for themselves. This means not wearing buttons or stickers showing support for a candidate (though apparel supporting issues or ballot measures are OK), keeping introductory comments evenhanded, and discouraging any derisive behavior in the audience. By demonstrating respect, you will earn more of it for your group.

Planning your forum, of course, involves including the media, which are often eager for access to candidates and the chance to see them in action with the community. Notify the press well in advance—send media advisories, make pitch calls, list the event on your local Associated Press daybook. Create press kits to distribute to reporters attending your event, and be sure to include the speaker line-up, a list of predetermined questions you may have for the candidates, and, of course, plenty of information about your organization and the issues you work on. Help the media understand the salience of your issue in the context of the campaign.

Think of your forum as the foundation for future policy advocacy and decision-maker accountability efforts. It's a first step in developing a relationship with someone who very soon might hold considerable power over the policies concerning your issue. Have someone take detailed notes on what the candidates say for future accountability sessions (or tape the event). Take good photographs for use in organizational materials or for your archives.

CANDIDATE FORUM CHECKLIST

☐ **Assemble your team**
Will this be a coalition effort among several groups, or will it be done by your group alone? Who is ultimately responsible for the coordination and implementation of the effort?

☐ **Determine your target(s)**
Which elected officials have the power to get you what you want? Draw up a list of all candidates running for the office(s) that hold sway over your issue. Be prepared to invite all major candidates for each office you select.

☐ **Set a date and location**
Think about what will maximize participation of your constituency—and the media: time of day, day of week, the location's accessibility, and occupancy limits.

☐ **Invite the candidates**
Do this as far in advance as possible. To increase the chance of acceptance, if possi-

ble, have someone connected to both the candidate and your group issue the invitation. Let the candidate know that their opponent has been invited (and whether they've accepted yet). The law is unclear on whether a 501(c)(3) forum can proceed if all the major candidates do not accept your invitation, so get legal advice if you find yourself in that situation.

☐ **Develop your format**
Discuss the following needs: ground rules, moderator, special guests or speakers (other than the candidates). Recruit people as needed to fill the roles. Decide on the format: Candidates can be given a set time to give their own remarks (usually three to seven minutes), and take questions from the audience at the end; candidates can be asked only questions developed by the group without making their own statement; or some combination. Let the candidates know the format, the time when they are scheduled to speak, and their time limits in advance.

☐ **Develop a budget and timeline**
List all the costs you anticipate (photocopying, supplies, postage, refreshments, etc.) and sources of funds. Develop a detailed monthly and weekly schedule of all activities into a master calendar.

☐ **Recruit volunteers**
How many volunteers will be needed for this total effort? Think through publicity, turnout, set-up and clean-up, hospitality (greeters and refreshments), child care, transportation, language translation, note-taking, photography. What is your plan to recruit these volunteers?

☐ **Obtain supplies**
Decide what you'll need, such as name tags, pens, sign-in sheets, tables for literature, refreshments, and child-care supplies. Do you need a sound system? Podium?

☐ **Develop a turnout plan**
Techniques for bringing in an audience can include word-of-mouth, organiza-

Town Hall meeting, Warren, Vermont. Photo: Hiroji Kubota/Magnum

tional mailings, inclusion in other groups' newsletters, announcements at other groups' or community meetings or at churches and synagogues, flyers, e-mail, phone banks, news releases, calendar listings in local media, etc. Plan to contact your own members personally, securing their commitments to attend. Follow up with reminders and transportation.

□ **Maintain good records**
Keep track of names and contact information for everyone who attends so you can include them in future efforts.

□ **Debrief**
Have a scheduled time to talk with your participants about what they learned about the candidates and the political process. Reinforce the ways your group expects to advance its goals through participation in the political process. Use the momentum and interest generated by the forum as an opportunity to sign people up for the next activity.

□ **Send thank-you's**
Follow up with thank-you notes to special guests or speakers, volunteers, donors of any goods or services, and the candidates (make sure not to imply endorsement if your group is a 501(c)(3) or if you haven't formally taken such a position as a 501(c)(4)).

RAPID RESPONSE TO CONVENTIONS

By Robert Bray

The Republican and Democratic national conventions, slated for New York and Boston respectively, offer grassroots activists an opportunity to hook their local news to the national action. Yes, these mega-media circuses can shut out the rest of us back home, but you can still respond to news happening at the events—and insert a local message.

Here are some tips for using the conventions as a news hook to highlight your issue.

- Are any delegates attending from your area who connect to your issue? Perhaps aim for a profile on them in the hometown paper, with a message about your issue included.

- For reporters covering the conventions, offer advance briefing on any local hooks. Get into their Rolodexes before the big events and let them know you are standing by to offer local commentary.

- Focus on a "message of the day" strategy. The conventions are often staged to drive one message every day, such as "Jobs and America," or "America and Security." If the day's theme is relevant to your issue, plan on responding with an appropriate message of your own tied into the conventions' message du jour.

- Have a nonpartisan response prepared and send it out immediately after keynote speeches. This is particularly true for the main speech by the successful nominee (the "balloon drop" speech). Offer local color in response to these big speeches, which are often the only things actually covered in prime time. Make sure your nonpartisan responses are also on your Web site.

- Connect your issue to any nonpartisan protests, rallies, or other events that are appropriate. If you have coalition partners who will attend and participate in outside activities at the conventions, let reporters know of the connections. Or perhaps someone from your own organization will be there. Consider pitching that person as an on-site media contact.

- Pitch an op-ed to the newspaper in advance of the convention that, again, localizes the big political themes to your area and issue. For example, "security" will be a major convention theme. Frame your domestic social change work—immigrant rights, deficit spending, whatever—into the dominant frame of "security," then communicate that in an op-ed.

- Be on standby to reporters. Let them know you are available for commentary on the issues as they unfold during the conventions.

photovault.com

IN THE SHADOW OF GROUND ZERO:

ACCOUNTABILITY CAMPAIGN SPEARHEADS A STRONG MESSAGE OF SOCIAL CHANGE AT THE GOP CONVENTION IN NEW YORK

The nation's political media attention will be on New York City during the Republican National Convention, as President Bush makes his reelection bid on the grand stage of Ground Zero. But that won't be the only news drama happening in town.

If plans go well, thousands of newly registered voters, labor representatives, clergy, social change advocates, and regular New Yorkers of every stripe will come together to communicate their messages under a new coalition effort called the Accountability Campaign 2004.

The Accountability Campaign will help bring together major New York City women's groups, trade unions, educators, religious leaders, civil libertarians, environmentalists, immigrant advocates, and social service providers. The Campaign is a 501(c)(4) coalition effort by more than 50 New York–based organizations to hold national leaders accountable in areas of urgent importance, such as assuring quality education and health care, providing full employment, protecting privacy and the right to choose, preserving civil liberties and immigrant rights, and conducting a responsible foreign and military policy.

The Accountability Campaign will support constituent groups in their efforts to expand voter registration and voter participation, with particular attention to the efforts of unions and religious organizations throughout the metropolitan region. The Accountability Campaign will assist its coalition partners in organizing effective, creative, nonviolent events, and provide media support for such events. It will act as a clearinghouse for its members' activities, organizing media briefings, photo ops, press conferences, rallies, and other newsmaking events before, during, and after the GOP Convention.

Organizers are well aware of the symbolic backdrop that Ground Zero offers the GOP convention, which will conclude with huge fanfare on September 2, just in time for Labor Day. They strongly believe the voices of regular New Yorkers affected by the tragedy and by the current economic situation should be heard.

"There is widespread concern over potential abuses of the terrible tragedy that was 9/11," said Rev. Peter Laarman, who stepped down as senior minister of Judson Memorial Church in New York to become the Accountability Campaign's chair. "We will call upon all national leaders to take great care against misappropriating our collective grief and loss.

"Our campaign's primary goal is to create communications channels and opportunities for vast numbers of everyday New Yorkers to become part of the national conversation on security and democracy," Laarman added.

To this end, the Accountability Campaign will seek to link the responses of ordinary New Yorkers to the convention in ways the news media will notice and report. One of the Campaign's task forces is focused on a project called "Sacred Memories." This project brings together Ground Zero survivors, family members, workers involved with demolition and rescue work, first responders, and concerned religious leaders. Well in advance of the GOP convention, these people will tell their stories and share their points of view with media representatives who are preparing "scene-setter" pieces on the convention.

Major New York constituencies concerned about "Americans Left Behind" will come together for a massive public demonstration spearhead by the Accountability Campaign on September 2 before the nominating convention concludes. New York's powerful labor movement plans to ask its members to march on September 2, which will replace the regular Labor Day commemoration in New York this year.

The Accountability Campaign is reframing the discourse that usually accompanies the circus-like setting of a national political convention. "At a time when this great city is likely to be used cynically as a stage set, we want to stand up for core values, like community and shared progress," said Laarman. "We want the rest of the country to see that we in New York City share the same Main Street concerns about the direction of the country that folks are feeling in Sheboygan and St. Louis and San Antonio—and that although we were hit by a great tragedy, we haven't lost our common sense about what really makes our nation strong."

Learn more about the campaign at www.accountabilityny.org.

NOT JUST ANOTHER BOSTON TEA PARTY:
SOCIAL FORUM AIMS TO CAPTURE SOME OF THE SPOTLIGHT AT DEMOCRATIC CONVENTION

Exciting opportunities are emerging in spring and summer 2004 to move a message of social change at the Democratic National Convention (DNC) in Boston.

The nonpartisan Boston Social Forum (BSF), to be held July 23–25 at the University of Massachusetts at Boston, immediately prior to the DNC kickoff on July 26, will gather thousands of activists from academic, cultural, and faith-based arenas. The purpose of the forum, according to BSF coordinator Jason Pramas, is to encourage various social movements to exchange information, network, form alliances, and communicate messages to the media attending the DNC. This is the first time the Democrats have held their convention in Boston. Some 15,000 media members are expected and the local community wants to seize the historic moment.

Pramas says organizations and advocates concerned with immigrant rights, racial and economic justice, the environment, housing, labor, communities of color, and numerous other issues have had input in planning for the forum. The three-day event will include workshops, plenaries, caucuses, and a visibility action, possibly a procession around the convention site.

"Many of the delegates attending the DNC come from diverse backgrounds—including gays and lesbians, unionists, feminists, and many others," says Pramas. "We want to show the Democrats, the media, the people of Boston, and the country a positive vision for change."

Meanwhile, a coalition of community-based groups is forming to explore additional opportunities to use the convention news hook to highlight their issues. Visit www.bostonsocialforum.org for more information on the BSF. Also, watch www.justicewithpeace.org, www.unitedfor peace.org, and www.veteransforpeace.org for links to other groups and details as they emerge.

Robert Bray is Founding Director and Senior Consultant at the SPIN Project, a nonprofit group of communications specialists who provide capacity-building to nonprofit public-interest organizations across the nation.

BIRD DOGS ON THE CAMPAIGN TRAIL:
HOLDING CANDIDATES ACCOUNTABLE

By Holly Minch

Throughout the election cycle, accountability opportunities abound. Bird-dogging is a tried-and-true—and fun!—method of highlighting your issue and holding candidates accountable. You can make your accountability efforts highly visible by asking your key questions of candidates in a public venue, in the eyes of their fellow citizens and, just as importantly, in the presence of the media.

Bird dogs frequent such locales as candidate forums, town hall events, candidates' stump speeches, and other public events where the media will be present to cover the race. Because most bird-dogging is done at candidate events, you are often letting the campaign do the work of turning out the media; you show up to help shape the story. Bird-dogging can be a chance to share the story—and, at best, the shot—with the candidate, if done well. If your organization can become the story by getting your message into the candidates' photo op, you become a part of the power landscape that shapes the debate on the issues.

But a word to the wise about the changed 2004 environment: If you are planning to push for candidate accountability in the presidential race, be prepared for heightened security and an uphill climb to get in front of the media.

501(c)(3) DOGGIES			501(c)(4) DOGGIES
Having a highly visible contingent from your organization at all public events of all candidates in a race (carrying signs, wearing T-shirts, etc.). This is a great way to publicly demonstrate your organization or community's support for an issue.	Planting a balanced question about your issue with reporters and encouraging them to pursue all the candidates for an answer.	Consistently asking all the candidates yourself, at various public appearances, the same balanced question about their position on your issue.	Asking candidates to pledge to support or oppose a certain legislative action once they are elected.

Bird-Dogging Pros

- Highly visible

- Can be a tool to keep your issues front and center in the mix of campaign issues

- Can be a light-hearted and fun way for volunteers to stay engaged in election-year efforts

Bird-Dogging Cons

- These are confrontational tactics, and they can damage your organization's future relationships with decision makers

- If your tactics are too confrontational, the action can backfire and turn voter sympathies to the candidate

- Requires infrastructure and resources for rapid response

- Unless carried out carefully and in a neutral manner, and directed equally at all candidates in a race, it can get 501(c)(3) organizations in hot water

The Bird-Dogging Spectrum

Some people think of bird-dogging as bedevilment—a kind of "unwelcome" committee. And indeed it can be. But there is a range of ways to present your bird-dogging efforts. The most important thing for a bird dog to remember is that your organization has to work with these people if they win. Sure, turn up the heat—but think carefully before you burn any bridges! And remember that only the mildest forms of bird-dogging can be engaged in by 501(c)(3)s—anything intended to embarrass a candidate would be off-limits.

Bird-dogging should never be the only item in your bag of tricks—but it can be a complement to other strategies and tactics you've used throughout the election year.

501(c)(4) DOGGIES

Carrying signs at public events that state the candidate's position on issues, and offering handouts to back up your statements ("Senator Rye voted against affordable housing 11 times") with a fact sheet documenting their voting record in office. Note: campaign staff will very likely try to remove you from the event, so have a backup plan.	Creating a highly visible mascot to follow a candidate to all their events. (In 1996, Buttman—a giant walking cigarette—followed Senator Bob Dole on his presidential campaign, to highlight Dole's acceptance of Big Tobacco campaign contributions. The media went wild, and Buttman dominated several news cycles' worth of coverage.) See previous column re: event ejection.	Disrupting a candidate event or staging a protest in front of a candidate's office. (Not recommended! Likely to draw more attention to the candidate than to your issue—and the news coverage is likely to paint your organization as a "rag-tag band of extremists.")

LICENSE TO BIRD-DOG: TIPS FOR ACTION

TO BIRD-DOG OR NOT TO BIRD-DOG

Some things to consider before taking a bird-dog action:

- What do you have to lose? Bird-dogging is confrontational, and you don't want to publicly embarrass someone when you might have been able to negotiate what you wanted in an amicable way. Plan your bird-dogging with an eye to the future.

- Are you sure? If you can't back up your claim, if you haven't double- and triple-checked your facts, you're not ready to bird-dog.

- Need to set the record straight? Bird-dogging is a great way for 501(c)(4)s to publicly correct the record when a candidate or elected official makes a false claim.

- Has a candidate done something good on your issue? Let the world know it, if you are a 501(c)(4). Your allies are likely to appreciate a public thank-you on the issues that have broad support in the community.

- Is it too quiet out there? If a candidate or elected official is dragging their feet on addressing an issue of importance, asking pointed questions in a public setting can force them to take a stance or take action.

Be prepared to move quickly

Because bird-dogging is more reactive than proactive, you often don't have much time to organize. You will need to quickly mobilize activists to attend candidates' events and rallies—and for 501(c)(3)s, that means treating all candidates in a race equally. Be prepared with efficient media lists, activist e-mail lists, and phone trees—and have these communication systems in place *before* you need them.

Humor is your friend

The best bird-dogging is funny and light-hearted while still delivering your message. If your bird-dogging methods are overly confrontational or too pointed, the news story—and voter sympathy—will tend to focus on candidate reaction to your means, not your message. But when it's funny—well, no one likes a public figure who can't take a joke.

Fetch yourself a schtick

If you are planning a sustained bird-dog effort, a prop or mascot can increase visibility with the media (and the candidate). Having a mascot, or large and colorful prop—a là Buttman—can help you drive your message home again and again. Make it tall, make it colorful, make it so nobody, especially the cameras, can miss it! Extra points if the candidate reacts or responds to your schtick in front of the press.

State the facts

Always back up your claims with hard facts, preferably those that are documented in public record or neutral, third-party sources such as newspaper articles. Show up with a press release or fact sheet that documents your claims, and distribute it to the press and others at the event. Having a press release or fact sheet ready for events is easy and essential. It must be on message and have quotable lines—the press loves a good sound bite! Be sure to quote your organizational leaders, and include a citation for all of your facts to document each of your claims. Be sure the release includes your contact info as well, so the media can follow up with you later.

Stick to the issue

Remember that 501(c)(3) organizations cannot support the election or defeat of any candidate. But you can focus on issues that are debated in the campaign. So focus your message and all your materials on the issue—not on a vote for or against the candidate.

Be timely

When President Clinton signed new health standards on smog and soot in 1997, a group of grateful bird dogs arranged to greet his plane just two hours after he signed the law, with a banner reading "Now we can all breathe easier—Thank You, President Clinton." They were cited in many of the news stories written about the new standards, and their photo ran alongside those stories in several papers. Quick turnaround pays off! (This kind of praise may have been suspect for a 501(c)(3) if 1997 had been an election year, so check to see how these rules apply to you this year.)

Get noticed

Yes, you represent a well-known, credible organization, and therefore you don't want to be so disruptive that you could be dismissed as a bunch of hotheads. But a big crowd, good visuals, and a good chant can make the difference between headline news and the newsroom recycling bin. Be creative, but don't make it so complicated that people can't catch your message.

Take the credit for a job well done

Make sure the candidate knows it was your organization that brought key issues to the forefront. This increases your political clout and reminds decision makers that as long as you are around, the bird dogs will be barkin'!

A GOOD BIRD DOG IS ALSO A WATCHDOG

Many bird-dogging opportunities go by with no action because we just plain miss them. To stay on top of every word a candidate speaks is impossible; to stay of top of most of them, however, is essential. Here are some ways to do that:

Monitor the candidates

- Treat candidates equally, whether they support or oppose your issue
- Catch television coverage and political ads
- Attend candidate events and forums
- Clip newspaper articles in which candidates make claims or promises on your issue
- Check candidates' Web sites regularly for position papers, text of speeches, and scheduled public appearances.

Make sure it all checks out

- Investigate all claims and promises—assume nothing
- Research candidates' records on all issues of concern to your group

Use the resources at your disposal

- Other local volunteers
- Local media
- Colleagues and allies

Respond quickly

- Draft a letter to the editor or an op-ed piece
- Call the reporter covering the story
- Be creative, but get it in the news!

BIRD-DOGGING CASE STUDY: MONEY WATCH 2000

By Holly Minch

Here's an example of a nonpartisan collaborative effort that was developed to capitalize on the New Hampshire primaries and the Iowa caucuses in 2000—two important early benchmarks in the election-year news cycle.

In 1999, the Iowa Citizen Action Network joined forces with their New England counterpart, the New Hampshire Citizens Alliance, to form Money Watch 2000, a collaboration designed to launch campaign finance issues onto the national radar screen.

Both groups counted on their states' prominence in the electoral process—and therefore the news cycle—to attract attention to their issues. The groups shared information and coordinated their efforts to get visiting journalists and candidates talking about public financing and other alternatives to big-money politics-as-usual. By working together, the two groups were able to make their message and their constituents' voices louder and clearer to the candidates—and the nation.

The groups' goals were clear and simple: They wanted to educate the public about their issue and raise the profile of campaign finance reform so that candidates had to address the issue during the nomination process in Iowa and New Hampshire. The increased political and media activity in communities in both states provided fertile ground.

The group was also wise in framing the issue. They focused not on campaign finance reform broadly, but on the specific need for public funding of elections. A key measure of their success was in getting candidates and the media to use their frame and their language on the issue. Candidates moved from talking about McCain-Feingold-type reform to directly addressing public funding. They were spurred as well by a reliable poll demonstrating that 74 percent of New Hampshire voters supported public financing of elections.

The real power of Money Watch 2000 was that candidates were bird-dogged (that is, trailed by activists and repeatedly asked the same questions) in both Iowa and New Hampshire.

Hearing the same message over and over made candidates feel that they had to respond, that they would be facing this issue in all states.

And unlike some bird-dogging efforts, Money Watch 2000 did not rely solely on opportunist media coverage. The group planned ahead for their media opportunities, anticipating ready-made news hooks, such as the quarterly campaign finance reporting periods. They worked directly with the media through editorial board meetings, op-eds, and so forth—and even did a training for reporters from more than 50 different media outlets on how to research and cover campaign finance issues. They got to know the national reporters covering the campaigns.

Money Watch 2000 also linked their earned media coverage to solid grassroots organizing efforts, including house parties, and intensive candidate education activities. They systematically trained grassroots spokespeople to stay on a very simple, clear message about the need for public funding.

Their hard work paid off. In January 2000, almost 800 Iowans went to their caucuses calling for comprehensive campaign finance reform. Their resolution was adopted in 475 caucuses covering 70 of Iowa's 99 counties. For their counterparts in New Hampshire, a key measure of success was that candidates who supported public funding did well in their races, which paved the way for further funding reform milestones: In 2000, "Clean Elections" legislation passed in the New Hampshire Senate and came very close to passing in the New Hampshire House of Representatives. Similar legislation establishing voluntary public financing of elections in New Hampshire was introduced in the state Senate in 2002—stay tuned for more in 2004!

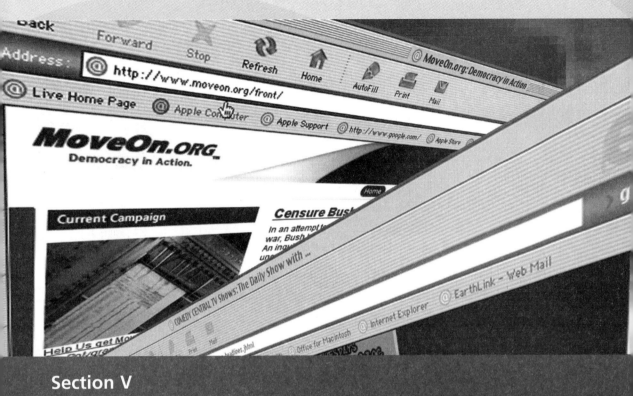

Section V

EMERGING
STRATEGIES

You've got to go deeper if you want to do more in 2004. It's not enough just to make it on the six o'clock news. Increasing numbers of Americans rely on alternate news sources—for better or worse, Jon Stewart's *The Daily Show* and Rush Limbaugh's programs are regarded as primary news sources by many younger voters. The Internet provides another medium that many are tuning in to. You need to be familiar with, and able to access, tools and technologies that will help you communicate either broadly though paid media or intimately through e-mail and the Internet. This section gives you examples of how to broaden your reach.

USING INTERNET TOOLS
TO EXPAND YOUR AUDIENCE, CAPACITY, AND LEVERAGE

By Greg Nelson

A s this book makes clear, a presidential election year presents numerous opportunities for nonprofit organizations to gain visibility for their issues, particularly through the media. While developing your strategy for 2004 and beyond, incorporating the use of Internet tools— from e-mail to online communities to web logs (or blogs)—into your planning is vitally important. The success of MoveOn.org's online movement-building and Howard Dean's early fundraising shows us that these tools can be used to achieve the basic goals of advocacy:

- Engaging and educating the general public
- Recruiting and retaining new members or supporters
- Building and deepening relationships with members and supporters
- Informing and influencing the press and other opinion leaders

This article presents some basic Internet tools and election-year programs that can greatly enhance and support the rest of the work you do.

Your Internet strategy should be designed much the same as any other component of your organization's work, such as direct mail or field work: as an integral element. Like other components, your Internet strategy should derive from your organizational goals and mission. Fundamentally, the Internet is just a new way to communicate with and connect to your members, potential supporters, and other target audiences, including the media and donors.

Where to Start

There is one thing every group must do: collect e-mail addresses. This means having an e-mail sign-up on your Web site, even if it's just for sending users periodic news updates, and a place for a supporter to record their e-mail address on all your donation materials, meeting sign-in sheets, and the like. What you do online will only be as good as how widely you can get your message out. Compiling a list of your supporters' e-mail addresses is therefore essential. The Dean campaign's growth, for example, exactly mirrored the growth of their e-mail list.

If you need a free or low-cost method for managing your e-mail lists, there are some basic resources available. Start by checking out the great bulletin boards and how-tos at TechSoup (www.techsoup.org). Many organizations choose Yahoo Groups (http://groups.yahoo.com) as a free list manager, and there are several inexpensive options as well, including the full-featured "E-mail Now" product from Groundspring (www.groundspring.org).

Set Your Priorities Based on Your Mission

In deciding how an online strategy and Internet tools might help you, identify which aspects of your organizational priorities could be accomplished online without dramatically altering what your organization is or how you do your work.

ESSENTIAL TIPS

You don't have to have it all figured out to get started. Too many groups wait until they completely understand this new medium before taking some basic steps. Start by collecting e-mail addresses, and get an e-mail list management platform and a privacy policy.

Organizations with different missions have different success factors—a group educating schools about HIV/AIDS may measure success by the number of curricula downloaded, while a group focused on securing additional funding for HIV/AIDS programs may track numbers of letters sent to key decision makers and dollars raised.

Take Advantage of the Attention

If you anticipate your issue or audience becoming an election-year issue, prepare for the additional attention you might receive by revamping the look of your Web site and highlighting the focused issue. A good example is the Violence Center's Campaign to Ban Assault Weapons (www.banassaultweapons.org), focused on renewing the assault weapons ban passed in 1994. They decided to do a campaign site because they anticipate the ban becoming an issue in the presidential campaign—as well as other federal races—and wanted to provide a one-stop shop for activists and donors to learn more about the issues and get involved in efforts to pass legislation. 501(c)(3) organizations should be careful about creating election-year pages that refer to candidates, though. (See Section 2 and the scorecards portion of Section 4 for guidance.)

Publicize Your Offline Programs

One of the most fundamental online activities is to publicize your offline events and programs. Online calendars—on your organization's site and public sites, such as your local newspaper—are among the most visited pages on any Web site. If you are planning a town hall meeting, a media event, or a rally, the Internet is a fantastic communications and distribution mechanism. If you are planning a nonpartisan candidate forum or an event to release a report, be sure to publicize it on your Web site, announce it to your e-mail list, and ask other organizations and the news media to publicize the event to their e-mail lists and on their news calendars.

Flash Campaigns

Flash campaigns are usually quick-hitting campaigns that last no more than a year. It's an appropriate strategy for promoting one particular issue above the rest of your work. The goal is to try to get news coverage, online coverage (e-mail lists, news services, listservs, blogs), and e-mail sign-ups in support of your issue.

A flash campaign usually consists of these components:

- A title reflecting your issue and position

- A catchy URL that ideally includes part of the chosen title

- A stand-alone Web site (or a specific section of your current site)

- An e-mail list for doing follow-up

- An online organizing plan to get the word out and keep people coming back

In order to make a splash, the content of the site often needs to be a little edgy. You don't need to go over the line or drift from your overall organizational tone and message, but think of a flash campaign as the rhetorical hot spot within your organization's message.

Here are some good examples of recent flash campaign sites:

- The Computer Takeback Campaign's Toxic Dude site (www.toxicdude.com)

was created to pressure computer manufacturers to recycle old computers so that they don't end up in landfills. The campaign utilized two strategies: ToxicDude.com targeted Dell Computers in particular with strong messages about corporate responsibility. The site stayed narrowly focused on generating online and offline activity with college students. Another site, ComputerTakeback.com, served as a more neutral nexus for basic information about the overall issue of computer recycling. Thus the campaign had two "faces" that raised awareness and generated action among different target audiences.

- ACORN's "Don't Be a Blockhead" campaign sought to pressure H&R Block to change the way they market their services to low-income people. The company provided instant cash to tax filers who were entitled to earned income tax credit but withheld half of the funds due to these taxpayers as a fee for the service. Dontbeablockhead.com exposed H&R Block's marketing practices. Combined with a canvassing and direct action strategy in multiple cities, the campaign provided several useful hooks for media. The site enhanced the scope and audience for the campaign, encouraging people across the country (not just in the geographic areas where ACORN was working on the ground) to get involved. This strategy turned a couple of local stories into a potential national story.

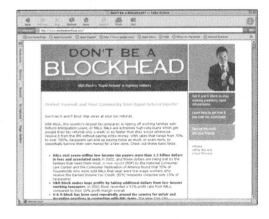

New Tools

Recently, several new tools—both commercial and non-commercial—have become crucial Internet-based mechanisms for organizing and for distributing information. These include Web logs ("blogs"), online voter registration, and social networking.

Blogs

One of the easiest to use, but most important, strategies is Web logs, more commonly referred to as "blogs." Blogs are essentially online journals that are managed, organized, and made available through the Web. The key to blogs is that they're easy to administer (no technical knowledge necessary). They can be updated frequently, and most blog services automatically allow posts to be archived, searchable, and categorized for easy reference. A good primer on blogs can be found in the how-to pages at www.techsoup.org.

Blogs are powerful because, when used well, they help to create community and bridge the space between an organization and its supporters. Because of their regular and informal nature, blogs are naturally a more personal medium. A well-crafted blog can help keep your supporters informed about your campaigns and organizations, and the ability for users to post responses allows you to get quick feedback and helps your supporters to feel involved.

The most popular blogging sites and software can be found at www.blogger.com and www.typepad.com.

Online Voter Registration

In large part because of the requirements of the Help America Vote Act (HAVA), there is now a national voter registration form (see www.fec.gov/votregis/vr.htm for details). As a result, national online voter registration (or at least the ability to fill out the form online) is possible, and several organizations are sponsoring large registration drives to help increase voter participation this year.

501(c)(3) groups should take care to ensure that all voter registration efforts are nonpartisan. If your organization does voter registration, it is worth looking at these groups as a potential resource (check that your state accepts the national voter registration form):

- **Working Assets' Your Vote Matters:** www.yourvotematters.org
- **Rock The Vote:** www.rockthevote.org
- **Declare Yourself:** www.declareyourself.org
- **Earth Day Network:** www.earthday.net
- **National Hip-Hop Political Convention:** www.hiphopconvention.org

MeetUp.com

The commercial site MeetUp.com received a lot of press in 2003 because of the success that presidential campaigns—particularly Howard Dean's—had in using the www.meetup.com Web site as a national organizing tool. The hype notwithstanding, MeetUp is a potentially powerful organizing tool, especially if your organization does national, statewide, or regional organizing and needs a method for arranging and promoting those efforts. In addition, MeetUp has established monthly events in every congressional and most state legislative districts. These events might be a great place to bring your own materials to help ensure that your issues are appropriately considered and debated during the election.

Social Networking Tools

New to the scene in the last year or two are a few "social networking tools," most of which are commercial but might still have online organizing value. These tools allow users to set up personal profiles (name, age, likes, dislikes, photos) and to find other people with similar interests, geographical proximity, or shared social networks. Use of these sites goes beyond looking for dates, as users connect with each other individually or with different "groups" or "interests." Once you're connected to those groups, you can subscribe to get newsfeeds, meet other individuals with the same interests, post to a common bulletin board, etc. Here are some examples of these sites:

- **www.friendster.org**
- **www.tribe.net**
- **www.ryze.com**

How do these social tools make sense for organizing? Organizing is fundamentally based on person-to-person interactions. At their best, these sites attempt to mirror the common interactions of day-to-day life: finding people of common interests so as to inspire, motivate, and achieve great things together.

What Does the Law Say about Online Activities?

In almost every way, the law about activities in an election year applies to online activities just as it does to offline ones. All of the same restrictions apply, and your communications, messaging, and coordination online will receive the same scrutiny (and perhaps more) as your offline work. There is, however, one major area where the Internet was given a pass. In the Bipartisan Campaign Reform Act of 2002, Internet communications were not included in the list of "public communications" that are restricted from TV and radio advertising by issue advocacy groups in the 60 days before an election. As a result, expect to see many organizations that are involved in the political cycle—from PACs to state parties and nonprofits—use Internet communications like e-mail and video streaming heavily in the final days of the 2004 election.

Ones to Watch

These groups are using the Internet creatively to organize and educate voters for the 2004 elections:

- **Working Assets' Your Vote Matters** (www.yourvotematters.org): Working to register 1 million voters.

- **Media for Democracy 2004** (www.mediafordemocracy.us): Citizen media watchdogs ensuring fair and balanced election coverage across the country.

- **Let's Talk America** (www.letstalkamerica.org): Conversations in communities across the country about what America is and what we as Americans want the country to stand for.

- **National Voice** (www.nationalvoice.org): A national coalition of nonprofit organizations working together to do more effective voter registration and field mobilization.

(ELECTRONIC) CIVIC PARTICIPATION

Despite evidence to the contrary, the myth persists that working-class voters can't be reached online. The idea that the Internet is the realm of freaks and geeks, Libertarians, Gen-Xs and Ys, and people too young to vote may have been true in 1995, but the online community has changed dramatically in the last decade.

- According to a summer 2003 NielsenNetRatings survey, an estimated 144 million adults 18 or older go online at least once a month, a figure almost as high as the estimated 150 million registered U.S. voters.

- According to a recent poll by the Online Publishers Association, Democrats and Republicans are online in equal numbers; nearly two-thirds of Internet users are over 35; and 42 percent have household incomes under $50,000 per year.

- Most notably, according to a 2002 study released by the Pew Internet & American Life Project, Americans are increasingly making the Internet their preferred means of community involvement and citizen participation.

Excerpted from "The Promise of the Internet for Ballot Measure Campaigns," by Roger Stone and Rob Stuart of Advocacy Inc. This article was originally published electronically by the Ballot Initiative Strategy Center.

Greg Nelson is a Partner and directs projects and business development for the political and Internet consulting firm Carol/Trevelyan Strategy Group (CTSG).

MoveOn.ORG
Democracy in Action.

CASE STUDY

MOVEON.ORG

By Don Hazen

By now, it seems that everyone has heard of MoveOn and their nationwide network of almost 2 million online activists. At the outset of the 2004 election cycle, MoveOn became one of the most recognized, effective, and responsive outlets for democratic participation.

The MoveOn phenomenon demonstrates a fundamental precept of online organizing, referred to sometimes as the Five C's: Connecting Computers Can Create Community. The best use of online communities such as MoveOn.org and MeetUp.com is to facilitate offline community building. The technology serves as a vehicle for people to make initial connections, but the power of these sites lies in what people do when they log off their computers and get together in the real world to work for social and political change.

Though MoveOn has invested in paid advertising in mainstream media to spread their messages, that's not the secret of their success. The limits of a blunt instrument like mass media advertising, especially on TV, are well known. As Lawrence Lessig, arguably the country's most innovative thinker about digital communication, explains, "Politics has always been about engaging people to act. For the past 50 years the most efficient tool for engaging people to action has been broadcast media. Yet over time people grow immune. When you're surrounded by images pushing every passion imaginable, the only sane response is to develop increasingly thick walls to block them out. As a result, broadcast has become increasingly weak...and the

weakened power of broadcast politics creates a strong incentive to develop an alternative."

MoveOn.org is one of the strongest of those alternatives, setting the standard for a new form of interactive politics in which the Internet and broadcast media combine to form a new approach to engage citizens. MoveOn's revolutionary potential lies in its ability to circumvent the corporate media with quality content that could potentially turn many of its members—and the larger group of families, friends, and colleagues they influence, potentially 10 million or more—into viral marketers.

The growth of the Internet has spawned a whole new class of super-communicators—individuals who have listservs and blogs and are the "viral" revolutionaries carrying the message of MoveOn and many other progressive Web sites. Many MoveOn members are influential in their communities. In the new communications parlance, they are "connectors," a term made famous by Malcolm Gladwell's book *The Tipping Point.* In *Unleashing the Idea Virus,* author Seth Godin calls them "sneezers." Whatever you call them, they are not shy about spreading their feelings to family and friends. They know that communication from a trusted friend or colleague is far more influential than a paid political advertisement or a direct market appeal.

Can substantial numbers of MoveOn members register voters, gather e-mail addresses, hold the corporate media accountable, and, perhaps most importantly, communicate a positive, clear vision of the future that is attractive enough to turn new voters out at the polls? Can this networked super-constituency evolve from well-informed financial supporters to election organizers? So far, so good.

In the last year, MoveOn has reached millions of people in their efforts to educate Americans on the issues. First, they launched an advertising campaign to urge U.S. leaders to "Let the Inspections Work" before waging war in Iraq. In addition to billboards and television ads, MoveOn ran ads in the *New York Times* to appeal to opinion leaders and the public. More than 10,000 MoveOn members got active in the campaign: They paid personal visits to their congressional representatives to urge them to vote against the war. They helped distribute more than 50,000 copies of Robert Greenwald's documentary *Uncovered*, which deconstructs the case for war in Iraq, by hosting more than 1,000 house parties and film screenings nationwide to share the film with family and friends. MoveOn also raised $10 million to purchase TV ads designed to educate the public about the impacts of tax cuts on the economy, jobs, and working families.

If they can do it, so can you! Here are a few lessons from MoveOn's success that can help your organization in action:

- Use online tools to grow your membership—and your clout!

- Activate your online supporters through real-world, local events and activities.

- Involve your members in selecting educational and political priorities—they are much more likely to engage with actions on issues they care about.

- Echo your messages by linking membership, field organizing, paid advertising, online strategies, and earned media.

- Encourage your members to communicate on your behalf—they can be your best messengers.

Don Hazen is Executive Director of the Independent Media Institute and Executive Editor of AlterNet. The Independent Media Institute (IMI) is a nonprofit organization dedicated to strengthening and supporting independent and alternative journalism and to improving the public's access to independent information sources.

SERIOUS IRREVERENCE:
THE DAILY SHOW BECOMES THE SOURCE FOR POLITICAL NEWS AND VIEWS FOR 2004

By Cynthia Moothart

Its own cheeky hype insists, "*The Daily Show with Jon Stewart* is the most important television show ever, with the most important guests, hosts, and news…of all time," while its host anchors a self-described "fake" news program and plays straight man to the day's events.

The show is embedded in such contradiction. Consider:

In mid-September 2003, U.S. Senator John Edwards (D-N.C.) formally announced his bid for the presidency while talking via satellite with Stewart. That same week Stewart interviewed former Secretary of State Madeleine Albright about her new memoir—the night before she appeared on NPR.

BETWEEN POLITICS AND THE PUNCHLINE

According to a January 2004 study from the Pew Center for People and the Press, 21 percent of Americans under 30 get their news from comedy shows such as *Saturday Night Live* and *The Daily Show*. This population cites these comedy shows as their regular sources for election news almost as frequently as they cite newspapers and evening network news programs.

The lesson for issue groups is this: The line between news and entertainment is blurring, and you can use this shift to invigorate the way your messages are received and understood among key audiences. With creativity and humor, your issues and ideas can walk that fine line between politics and the punchline.

Days later, *The Daily Show* won two Emmys for comedy. Just months earlier, the Television Critics Association had nominated the show for Outstanding Achievement in News and Information alongside *Frontline, Nightline,* and *60 Minutes.* (Resist the temptation to disregard TV critics as mere fans; the show also won a prestigious Peabody Award for its election coverage in 2000.)

While interviewing Stewart this summer on *NOW with Bill Moyers*, the veteran newsman confessed, "I do not know whether you are practicing an old form of parody and satire . . . or a new form of journalism." Moyers later added: "When I report the news on this broadcast, people say I'm making it up. When you make it up, they say you're telling the truth."

The million-plus nightly viewers who tune into *The Daily Show* on Comedy Central are college-educated thirtysomethings with salaries that exceed the national norm. Most viewers—62 percent—are male. The show continues to build audience within this key demographic, says Steve Albani, a Comedy Central spokesman, because it's relevant and irreverent.

"It's one of the few shows out there that can truly speak its mind on current issues," he says. "We often see a spike in viewers after major events; they want to know Jon's take on what they just saw. With 24-hour programs there's an increasing goal of getting news out there fast—oftentimes the news is put out before it's been confirmed or analyzed. *The Daily Show* peels away layers to see what's at the core. It doesn't go for the easy joke. It goes for the joke that makes you laugh and makes you think at the same time."

Cynthia Moothart is Managing Editor for Content at In These Times, *a national, biweekly magazine of news and opinion published in Chicago. This article is excerpted, with permission, from "Lessons from the Idiot Box," In These Times, 11/17/03.*

THE 2004 INDEPENDENT MEDIA LANDSCAPE:
HOW THE INTERNET CHANGES THE WAY WE COMMUNICATE

By Don Hazen

In the face of increasing media concentration and corporate media conservatism, independent media, especially on the Internet, have grown in influence and audience. This is good news for organizations that have an eye to the 2004 election.

Independent media sources are now able to reach millions of people in a multitude of ways, with highly trafficked Web sites, popular blogs, viral marketing, clever messaging, and symbolic online events. The Internet's e-mail capacity and the World Wide Web have been a blessing to political organizing. For example, without e-mail, it would have been extremely difficult to organize the powerful 1999 Seattle WTO demonstrations that woke the world up to the consequences of global trade. Of course, the early attention and impressive fundraising success that Howard Dean received in 2003 and 2004 was also largely the result of grassroots mobilization on the Internet.

Independent media have a key role to play in countering the noise of mainstream media in this election year. No longer limited to small magazines, public access TV, and small radio networks, the new alternative media are professional and compelling, with important stories to tell.

The Reach of Independent Media

In the face of a more conservative corporate media, there are positive independent media developments. The number of people being reached with public interest information has increased perhaps five-fold over the past five years. In the "old days" of primarily print magazines, direct mail, and very modest grassroots radio (NPR excepted), the independent media audience was in the range of 3 to 5 million, and many magazines were published monthly or even bimonthly. With the Internet, the audience has grown to 15 to 20 million, and news and analysis are available 24/7. A host of independent Web magazines typically can reach a million people a month or more.

The independent media old guard of print and radio remain influential, especially among older readers, and are also doing well, with increasing numbers of subscribers and listeners. Over the last five years, the independent media landscape had shifted dramatically: We've seen an increase in quality content and access to compelling information often unavailable in corporate media. Outspoken media figures like Michael Moore, Molly Ivins, Al Franken, Amy Goodman, Greg Palast, Robert Scheer, and many others have been helped by the Internet and the growing independent media infrastructure. When Palast was asked how his book *The Best Democracy Money Can Buy* rose to the *New York Times* bestseller list without being reviewed in any major daily newspaper, his response was, "The alternative media—but its name should be changed because it reaches more people than the mainstream."

With the large increase in Internet use as a key source of information for millions of people, there has been a breakdown of traditional news gatekeepers. Google and MoveOn.org, the blogging craze, AlterNet, One World, Work for Change, BuzzFlash, Truth Out, Grist, Common Dreams, Media Channel, True Majority, TomPaine, and many more are all experimenting and creating new media voices.

Many of these new media entities are doing serious thinking about models of collaboration and cross-marketing, and in some cases they are already working together to test assumptions and increase the reach of independent news and ideas. In important ways,

the Internet media revolution is the "other" media reform movement. Despite unprecedented public interest in a more democratic media, media reform in Washington has floundered due to the reluctance for change at the FCC and in the Bush administration, as well as heavy corporate media lobbying. With no real regulatory reforms in sight, and with the urgent need to get the word out in an election year, the immediate reform lies in creating and building an independent media infrastructure. The future holds the potential for an interconnecting independent network of radio, TV, print, and online media.

The Internet is not a panacea, however, as the Dean 2004 presidential campaign and MoveOn's futile attempt to slow Arnold Schwarzenegger's 2003 candidacy for governor of California demonstrated. Connecting people on the Internet can raise money, get the word out, and even help bring people together and create community. But what you do to keep them connected is crucial. And, of course, not everyone is computer-savvy and many people, particularly poor people, are not online.

How Can the New Media Bring New Voices to Elections?

In the context of elections, there are a number of key questions: How can the new media be best employed in the service of priority issues and values? How can non-profit organizations make better use of independent media or even make media of their own? Given that the majority of Americans support principles of fairness and equity, protecting the environment, and extending health care, how can we use new technologies to communicate these core values effectively? Can we help people feel that change is possible and that they are part of something larger, so that they ultimately go to the polls and encourage their family and friends to do so as well?

Here the Internet can help. One of the advantages of communicating digitally is that

REACHING YOUR AUDIENCE THOUGH THE INDEPENDENT MEDIA

How can your organization use new media and independent sources to educate voters on the issues this election year? Here are a few tips:

- Follow the coverage of your issue in the independent media. You can stay current with sources like AlterNet.org, CommonDreams.org, and TomPaine.com.

- Include independent online outlets on your media list; send them your press releases and story ideas.

- Alternative media tend to be highly segmented and can be a great way to reach very specific audiences. Find the outlets whose niche is your audience. How? By asking your members where they get their information.

- Since many independent media outlets are short-staffed, send them ready-to-use content, like op-eds. Many of these outlets would like to run coverage of the issue, but don't have a huge staff of writers to generate the stories—which means they may run your well-written commentary as is.

- Give independent sources lots of lead time. Remember that independent media are working on a wide range of publishing schedules—your issues are more likely to be covered if you give plenty of time for them to worked into the editorial line-up.

- Especially for online outlets, use e-mail pitches. Editors working on tight deadline with a short staff might not pick up their phone, but they are constantly looking at their e-mail.

you can control your own messages. Another is that groups can make easy alliances with allies to cross-promotion and to reach larger audiences cheaply.

The Big Campaign

This crucial election year will doubtless bring distorted mainstream coverage of campaigns and issues, as broadcast media become more ideological and mindlessly adversarial. Enormous amounts of money will be spent on a dizzying array of media ads, leaving much of the public alienated and confused.

The ever-escalating war of campaign dollars and dueling attack ads is a huge negative factor in American politics. In the 2004 elections, a number of dubious fundraising and campaign spending records will be broken. Record amounts of money will be raised and spent on campaign advertising, as personal attacks and distortions make it increasingly difficult for voters to distinguish what is in their social or economic interest.

In the end, voters' decisions may frequently be swayed by emotional issues, personalities, or ads, unless there is a potent counter force to carry an independent, critical perspective.

A 2003 study by the polling firm Knowledge Networks, working with the University of Maryland's Program on International Policy Attitudes, found that people who watch commercial television are much more likely to be misinformed than those who get their information from print media or PBS, NPR, and other independent sources. Another study from the Pew Center for People and the Press showed that people who get most of their information from the Internet are likely to be the most informed.

It is well known that negative political advertising is frequently designed to shrink the electorate, as it makes some people, especially those who are undecided, so disgusted with the endless attacks that they stay home on Election Day.

Implications for Community Advocates

Part of the job of communicators within nonprofit groups is to offer positive visions and hope in the face of what often can be nasty and confusing campaigning. The more people participate, particularly those who have been left out of the political process, the healthier our democracy.

Public interest groups—operating separately from parties and candidates—have a challenging task to answer inaccurate and distorted news coverage and propaganda ads with communication and information of their own. The hope is to provide enough public education via ads, the Internet, mail, and face-to-face contacts to preserve an environment in which people can be open

to alternative arguments. Those fighting for more truth and less distortion in the media are constantly struggling to keep pace with the information onslaught. Grassroots efforts must be employed to supplement and echo values driven messages, support voter registration drives, and raise awareness among voters.

Liberating public discourse from the constraints of consolidated corporate media will, of course, require concerted efforts by various stakeholders and constituencies over a long period of time. Nevertheless, a healthy and diverse media system is the best protection for an informed citizenry, facilitating the public's engagement in issues and enabling the voters to hold their elected officials accountable.

Don Hazen is Executive Director of the Independent Media Institute and Executive Editor of AlterNet. The Independent Media Institute (IMI) is a nonprofit organization dedicated to strengthening and supporting independent and alternative journalism, and to improving the public's access to independent information sources.

ARE BALLOT INITIATIVES PART OF YOUR POLITICAL TOOLKIT?

By Kristina Wilfore

Ballot initiatives have emerged as a new battleground in our national political debate. While many right-wing groups have used the initiative process very effectively, progressive organizations are only now starting to use ballot initiative efforts to complement their electoral and lobbying strategies.

Ballot initiatives that affect civil rights, reproductive freedom, workers' rights, the environment, and many more issues are expected to qualify in 2004. While tax law restricts 501(c)(3) organizations from electioneering for or against candidates, the law does allow public charities to work on ballot measures. There is no reason not to use this powerful tool to our advantage. If used strategically, ballot initiatives can embed progressive policies in state law and mobilize and energize activists to work for their values.

Staying Legal with Ballot Initiatives

Ballot measure activities by 501(c)(3) organizations are treated as lobbying, which is permissible for public charities, within limits. Even signature-gathering to put a measure on the ballot and paid ads that specifically advocates for a "yes" or "no" vote on a measure are considered lobbying under IRS rules.

HOW CAN NONPROFITS PUT INITIATIVES ON THE BALLOT?

Many states have a provision in their constitutions that allows for citizen-initiated ballot measures. There are many easy-to-understand steps in the process, and these differ by state. In general, sponsoring organizations must file an application with the secretary of state, obtain the required number of signatures, and adhere to all of the state's campaign finance regulations and timelines. For details on the specific requirements in your state, visit www.ballot.org and click on "In Your State."

Most states that do not allow citizen-initiated ballot measures do have provisions requiring that state legislators carry proposed constitutional amendments to the ballot on behalf of citizens. For contact information for election officials in your state, see www.ballot.org and click on "In Your State."

Many groups choose the "501(h) Expenditure Test" because it provides a clear definition of lobbying and limits. The 501(h) test allows 501(c)(3) organizations to spend as much as 20 percent of their exempt purpose spending on lobbying. At that 20 percent, 501(c)(3) groups can spend a quarter of their overall lobbying limit on grassroots lobbying (activities designed to encourage the general public to lobby elected officials directly). In order to use the "h" election standard, your group must fill out a one-time application (IRS Form 5768). For a thorough explanation of permissible lobbying activities, consult "Legal Issues for Nonprofit Advocates," by John Pomeranz, in *Grassroots Grants,* by Andy Robinson (Jossey-Bass, 2004). Under the "h" election standard, only *expenditures* for or against a ballot measure count as lobbying. As a 501(c)(3), therefore, you can safely spend up to your lobbying limit on ballot measures. You can spend even more if some activities do not count as lobbying under certain exceptions allowed by the IRS.

Furthermore, a number of activities related to ballot measures—like nonpartisan analysis, studies, and research—are considered educational, not lobbying. Therefore, 501(c)(3) funds can be raised and spent on non-lobbying communication like broadcast ads and direct mail without those expenditures counting towards 501(h) lobbying limits. Also, research and organizing that are not conducted primarily for use in lobbying do not count as a lobbying expenditures.

Also, charities need to comply with any state or local campaign finance laws that apply to ballot measures in their area. In California, for example, ballot measure campaigns are subject to extensive reporting requirements under the Political Reform Act.

SIGNS OF THE TIMES:

NEW INITIATIVES PROMOTE PEACE AND CIVIL LIBERTIES

In addition to the dozens of antiwar and anti–Patriot Act resolutions that have passed through city councils across the country, community advocates in California, Denver, Chicago, and in other parts of the country are turning to the ballot initiative process to further their agendas. An initiative in Alaska recently sought to appoint a task force to study and report on exemption from Selective Service registration; a Denver ordinance required the city to help ensure public safety by increasing peacefulness; and Chicago activists sought to address draconian aspects of the Patriot Act in order to raise the profile of civil liberties in Illinois.

For more information about using ballot measures to spotlight issues, see www.ballot.org.

For more information, contact:

Alliance for Justice
202–822–6070 or www.afj.org
Ballot Initiative Strategy Center
202–223–2373 or www.ballot.org

Kristina Wilfore is Executive Director of the Ballot Initiative Strategy Center, an organization committed to giving progressive activists the tools they need to wage effective campaigns. Information for this article was taken in part from "Seize the Initiative," a publication of the Alliance for Justice.

THE PROMISE OF THE INTERNET FOR BALLOT MEASURE CAMPAIGNS

By Roger Stone and Rob Stuart

In 2004, election victories will go to campaigns that master the Internet, and ballot initiative campaigns are no exception. Here is a list of quick tips to help you make the most of the Internet to maximize support for ballot measures that will advance your policy agenda:

- Collect e-mail addresses in every public action, event, appeal, and appearance.

- Be sure to include your organization's Web address on every piece of materials created for the campaign and include a field for e-mail addresses on every sign-in sheet.

- Solicit members of your coalition for their e-mail lists.

- Encourage your subscribers to take steps necessary to ensure delivery. Spam filters are becoming increasingly popular and are catching even desired mail.

- Personalize messages and include a compelling subject line.

- Messages should be reader-friendly, eye-catching, and not too heavy on text and should present a clearly defined request for action (donate funds, tell a friend, attend a rally, write a letter to the editor, host a house party, vote, etc.).

- Messages from your campaign should be timely. Communicate with your readers regarding a specific event, not simply because it is the 15th of the month.

- Messages should be focused on one theme, not an assortment of miscellaneous information.

- According to Internet experts, the day of the week that messages are sent also makes a difference. Readers are more likely to pay attention to an e-mail sent to them early in the week, as opposed to one sent on a Thursday or Friday.

- Create incentives or urgency for people to donate or to recruit others.

- Web sites are a great opportunity to impact a ballot initiative. Use your site to tell compelling stories and to highlight recent successes.

Roger Stone and Rob Stuart are based at Advocacy Inc., an Internet-based political and issue-oriented advertising firm. Advocacy Inc.'s services include electronic surveys, e-mail campaigns, and e-mail-list enhancement. See www.advocacyinc.com.

CASE STUDY

FLORIDA BALLOT INITIATIVE

By Gregory Joseph

Working for a living has long been a struggle for many Americans, with wage standards differing drastically from state to state and generally hewing to the low end of the spectrum. But community advocates in Florida have taken a proactive approach by launching an initiative for the November 2004 Florida ballot that would help guarantee an honest wage for honest work.

Strong lobbying from pro-business interests has kept Florida among one of seven states without a minimum wage. Now the Association of Community Organizations for Reform Now (ACORN) and a coalition of other community and labor organizations have drafted a state constitutional amendment that would set Florida's minimum wage at $6.15, benefiting all employees currently covered by the federal minimum wage.

"After years of inaction at the federal level, pushing for a higher minimum wage at the state and local level is the necessary alternative route to address the economic needs of low-income families," wrote the Brennan Center for Justice in New York City, which drafted the Florida ballot initiative and will serve as legal counsel for the effort.

ACORN's research shows that raising the minimum wage will improve the lives of lower-earning households. If Florida's ballot initiative passes, more than 300,000 workers will see higher wages as a direct result.

Overall, 67 percent of the gains from the proposed increase would go to the bottom 40 percent of households.

700,000 John Hancocks

Plenty of hurdles to getting the amendment on the ballot remain. The first step is collecting the 490,000 signatures required to propose the initiative for the November ballot. "We're actually aiming for 700,000" says ACORN's Brian Kettenring, of the number of signatures they will turn over to the Florida secretary of state's office by the August 2 deadline. "Submitting 700,000 gives us room to survive the inevitable challenges."

ACORN's signature drive will be fueled by a mix of highly trained political organizers, community leaders, and volunteers. Currently, 40 ACORN-trained organizers have taken up residence in the state, and paid canvassers have already created the crucial organizing structure in targeted communities. For Florida's March primary, ACORN

sought to recruit 2,000 volunteers to gather signatures at the polls, hoping to match the success of the Florida Education Asssociation, which gathered 400,000 signatures for a class-size initiative as voters cast their ballots in the November 2002 election.

In an effort to communicate their message, ACORN has also enlisted the assistance of numerous community and civil rights groups, the faith community, elected officials, and thousands of grassroots activists under the umbrella "Floridians for All." The groups have reached out to low-income workers who live in communities where much of ACORN's local work has taken place and who are expected to benefit from a minimum wage increase.

"ACORN is already in those communities," says organizer Renee Ruiz of ACORN's 30-year history of pushing issues for communities that are often ignored. There's a general feeling that their relationship to these communities will serve them well on this campaign, and it comes as no surprise that ACORN anticipates the deepest support to come from these neighborhoods.

Calling All Voters

ACORN is multitasking. The signature drive is coupled with a voter registration effort, which in January 2004 had already registered 13,000 new voters, largely low- and moderate-income African-American and Latino adults. ACORN expects to register a total of 100,000 African-American, Caribbean-American, and Latino voters over the course of the campaign. Carrying out this mission is a voter registration staff of 50, with each staff member responsible for registering 20 new voters a day.

The ACORN teams rely on time-tested practices to build their organization. It's not just signatures ACORN is gathering: After registering new voters, they also collect phone numbers and e-mail addresses to help them turn a signature into a vote on November 5. "With the proper follow-up, our research shows that 80 percent of the people who give a phone number are more likely to show up at the polls," says Kettenring. Not only will this practice help ensure voter turnout, but it also builds an ever-growing list of supporters and possible funders for ACORN. The effort in Florida will yield nearly 500,000 names and phone numbers and 140,000 e-mail addresses, providing ACORN with an invaluable network for the November general election ballot measure and beyond.

Paying particular attention to Florida's vast and diverse Latino community, ACORN staffed each of its seven offices across the state with bilingual workers. "Raising the minimum wage affects every demographic, in every age group," says organizer Ruiz, "and our staff reflects that." With the Latino community in mind, ACORN has held strategy and outreach meetings with respected organizations in the community, such as La Raza and the Orlando-based Latino Leadership.

Research shows that when the economy is stagnating, low-income voters often are discouraged from voting. ACORN hopes that the minimum-wage initiative will be an incentive for new voters to turn out in November, providing an increase in civic participation among low-income communities. When a minimum wage initiative appeared on a ballot in Washington state in 1998, it was credited with a 4 percent increase in voter turnout. Louise Peterson, ACORN chair for St. Petersburg, Florida, puts it this way: "In lower-income neighborhoods, we expect people to be eager to support this effort since they will have the chance to vote themselves a raise."

Women are a major target group for ACORN's goal of 100,000 new voters, as they stand to reap the greatest gains if the ballot initiative is passed. Women in Florida make up less than half the total workforce, yet 76 percent of households living on a minimum wage are headed by a woman.

ACORN has partnered with Voices for Working Families, Planned Parenthood, and numerous other organizations that stress a progressive agenda for women. ACORN is also working jointly with Florida's "welfare-to-work" community to educate working women that a dollar increase in their minimum wage means an extra $2,000 a year for a full-time worker or, as Kettenring told the *Orlando Sentinel* last year, with the extra dollar "someone could maybe go to night school or buy that house instead of renting for the next ten years." Josh Myles, state political coordinator for ACORN, summed it up when he said that more money in your paycheck means more money for "food, housing, and electricity."

ACORN hopes the appeal of this issue will help Florida take an important step toward providing economic equality for thousands of low-wage workers. With the experience of past community organizing successes under their belt and an ever-growing base of support, ACORN has set out to help Florida's working families secure their future.

Gregory Joseph is a contributor to AlterNet.org, an online magazine providing a mix of news, opinion, and investigative journalism on subjects ranging from the environment, the drug war, technology, and cultural trends to policy debate, sexual politics, and health.

LOCAL NETWORKING FOR NATIONAL MOVEMENT BUILDING:
IMMIGRANT WORKERS' FREEDOM RIDE

By Laura Saponara

Just as the Freedom Rides of the early 1960s exposed the brutality of racism and the power of organized resistance, the Immigrant Workers' Freedom Ride (IWFR) of 2003 focused public imagination on the injustice of U.S. policies toward immigrants. Nine hundred freedom riders from more than 50 nations traveled across the country to bring this message to Washington, D.C.: *The road to citizenship needs a new map.* Along the way, the riders brought their stories of hard work, hardship, and hope to millions of Americans. At the end point in New York, more than 100,000 people gathered to honor the Freedom Riders, the largest rally by and for immigrants in U.S. history.

More than a series of events, the IWFR was a means to movement-building, one that emphasized the power of immigrants to strengthen our democracy by participating in the electoral process.

The links between the IWFR and the civil rights movement were not merely rhetorical. The values and strategies of the civil rights movement were put into practice on the IWFR buses, where riders took part in his-

tory lessons on race relations, voting rights, and the role of immigrants in shaping U.S. democracy. Like the civil rights movement, the IWFR used themes, messages, and imagery that are distinctly American and distinctly moral. The result was a series of powerful frames familiar to reporters and readers. These frames were reinforced when Freedom Riders from the 1960s provided a historical hook by endorsing the IWFR and climbing aboard.

The Goal

A key goal of the IWFR media strategy was to counter the perception that only elected officials and dueling advocacy organizations care about immigration policy. By prioritizing local coverage, including ethnic media, IWFR strategists sought to demonstrate that there is a great deal of interest in immigration reform at the grassroots level. Community members *here* believe that undocumented workers should be entitled to legal status. Residents *here* care about the reunification of families separated by borders. *Our* community will stand up to press for workplace protection and civil rights for immigrants. If the media strategy succeeded, an impressive volume of coverage spanning the entire country would serve as evidence of broad popular support for the human rights of immigrants in the U.S.

The Strategy: A "Tsunami" of Local News Coverage

IWFR's strategy was to create a tidal wave of coverage that would begin as the buses launched from the West Coast and swell as the riders continued eastward. To make media happen, IWFR organized a nationwide grassroots structure of more than 100 media coordinators. In the cities where the buses launched, the media coordinators were charged with generating coverage of the kick-off events that heralded the start of the journey. Media coordinators in every host city along the way would bank on the buzz from prior coverage to target new reporters along the route. As the buses covered more and more miles, the media coordinators would seize more and more opportunities for coverage.

Media coordinators shouldered a huge amount of responsibility for the success of the media strategy. In the months and weeks before the ride began, media coordinators compiled media databases, prepared talking points and press packets, pitched stories, coordinated editorial board meetings, drafted op-eds, and booked riders on radio talk shows, among other duties.

The Launch

The groundwork laid by the media coordinators and IWFR's national communications staff began to pay off well before the first buses rolled. Early on, CNN, the *Miami Herald,* and the Spanish language network Univisión committed to following the story at length by embedding reporters with the riders for all or part of the journey.

Headlines of stories printed in the summer months prior to the ride reflected IWFR's key messages, such as, "Freedom Buses to Roll Again," (*Arizona Republic*, 6/28/03); "California Senate Backs Freedom Ride to Improve Immigrant Workers' Status," (*Los Angeles Times*, 6/27/03); "Supporters of Immigration Rights Will Take Fight to National Stage," (*Las Vegas Review Journal*, 8/13/03); and "Preparan Masiva March Pro Inmigrante" (Univisión Online, 6/27/03).

Ten days ahead, stories about the journey had already appeared in news reports in 19 states and in national media such as the U.S. government's Voice of America, the Associated Press, and Univisión Online.

The media campaign got a big boost when the buses launched from the West Coast on September 23. Associated Press wire stories propelled the ride to national news and served as a heads-up to reporters across the country that the riders would soon be coming their way. As word spread, reporters filed advance stories in the Midwest, South, and East. The number of hits to the IWFR website via Google increased exponentially as the territory covered by the buses expanded.

To complement the groundswell of coverage generated by the media coordinators, IWFR hired a private communications consulting firm to pitch stories to national media outlets, including television, and to write and place editorials and op-eds.

THIS IS WHAT "ON MESSAGE" LOOKS LIKE:

"The road to citizenship, the right of immigrant workers to reunite their families and protect their rights in the workplace…[these] are just basic human rights."
—Suzanne Murphy, organizer, Minneapolis, AP wire story, 2/2/03

"We'll gather to celebrate the rights and responsibilities as well as the gifts and talents that immigrant workers bring to this country and to their communities."
—Leo Anchondo, Office of Immigrant Concerns,
Catholic Diocese, Austin, *Austin American-Statesman*, 8/23/03

"We're hard workers. We pay taxes and we obey laws. We're here…and we want to be treated fairly."
— Mario Ramos, worker, *The Tenessean*, 9/2/03

"We may have come in on different boats, but if we don't keep fighting for civil rights, we're all going to sink on the same boat."
—Atlanta civil rights activist Rev. James Orange, *Denver Post*, 9/28/03

"They tell me this is the country of freedom. You're supposed to have the right to speak. But immigrants don't have the right to speak out on the job because they get fired."
—Federico Gonzales, *New York Times*, 9/28/03

"Your movement is our movement. No community can prosper where workers are exploited, undervalued, and underpaid."
—Jerry L. Helmick, United Food and Commercial Workers Union,
District Local No. 2, Kansas City, *Kansas City Star*, 9/29/03

Rolling with the Buses

The first buses rolled off from the West Coast (Seattle, Portland, the San Francisco Bay Area, and Los Angeles) on September 23. In the six days that followed, the ride launched from six additional cities - Las Vegas, Houston, Miami, Chicago, Minneapolis, and Boston. This meant that by September 28, when all of the buses were on the road, Freedom Riders would land in a total of 16 cities each day, presenting media opportunities in 62 cities over a five-day period.

Messages

The messages of IWFR were designed to draw attention to the injustice of current immigration policies and to convey solutions that invoke progressive American ideals. Let's think about these messages in terms of the SPIN Project's "Problem-Solution-Action" model. Because IWFR sought to change popular perceptions of immigrants but was not tied to a specific platform or legislation, here I've replaced "action" with "truth."

IWFR MESSAGES

THE PROBLEM:
Bad immigration laws harm good people.

- Our immigration system leaves some 8 to 10 million immigrants in the shadows, vulnerable to abuse and exploitation.

- By keeping immigrants in legal limbo, the system undermines the bargaining power and labor rights of all workers.

- Many immigrants are forced to live apart from loved ones for years, even decades.

THE SOLUTION:
The immigration system can be fixed with just laws and policies that strengthen America and reflect our ideals.

- **Reward work** by granting legal status to hard-working, tax-paying, law-abiding immigrant workers already established in the U.S.

- **Renew our democracy** by clearing the path to citizenship and full political participation for our newest Americans.

- **Restore labor protections** so that all workers, including immigrant workers, have the right to fair treatment on the job.

- **Reunite families** in a timely fashion by streamlining our outdated immigration policies.

- **Respect the civil rights and civil liberties of all** so that immigrants are treated equally under the law, the federal government remains subject to checks and balances, and civil rights laws are meaningfully enforced.

THE TRUTH:
Immigrants are new Americans who share our values and aspirations.

- Immigrant workers work hard, pay taxes, and sacrifice for our families.

- Immigrants care for our children, tend to our elderly, pick and serve our food, and build and clean our houses, among other underpaid, essential jobs.

- Immigrant workers living and paying taxes in the U.S. want to get on a path to citizenship, reunite with their families, have a voice on the job, and be treated fairly.

Synopsis of Media Coverage

The success of the IWFR media strategy speaks for itself!

- Substantial coverage of the ride in the form of feature stories or editorials appeared in 48 out of the top 50 newspapers in the U.S.

- More than 863 news stories were generated in print media across the country.

- The ride was featured or mentioned in 641 different English and Spanish language television news programs.

- Media in Great Britain, France, Germany, Switzerland, Jamaica, Taiwan, Philippines, Australia and South Africa covered the ride.

Eyes on the Prize

The Immigrant Workers Freedom Ride was a step—a giant step—in an ongoing struggle for equal opportunity, desegregation and equal rights under the law. The ride built trust and ties among people from different organizations and movements who had not worked together before and likely did not perceive the interconnections of their struggles. New immigrants who knew little about the civil rights movement were amazed to learn about the conditions of segregation endured by African Americans in the South. As they sat silently at infamous lunch counters in Mississippi and walked the campus of Central High School in Little Rock, the new Freedom Riders began to understand the courage and sacrifice that was required of activists in the civil rights movement, and to recognize the political effectiveness of collective action.

Similarly, African-American riders and residents of Southern host cities gained insights into the family histories, work lives, and cultures of immigrant workers from the Northwest, Midwest, Southwest and countless places in between. The NAACP joined with immigrants' rights organizations and labor unions to plan events in host cities.

At local levels, labor unions and Central Labor Councils participated side-by-side with immigrant rights organizations. These partnerships triumphed over initial challenges that stemmed from the economic disparity between unions and struggling, grassroots nonprofits that operate without a stable funding base. Labor leaders played leading roles *and* supporting roles, resulting in new relationships enlivened by trust.

How will the Immigrant Workers Freedom Ride continue to make history? In the post-Ride period, organizations in originating and host cities are already building upon the strength of coalitions formed during the ride. IWFR participants and supporters are advocating for the rights of immigrants in local and national policy issues ranging from the right to get a driver's license to access to higher education to the injustice of repressive legislation.

National labor leader Maria Elena Durazo was invited to participate in the annual celebration of the birth of the Rev. Martin Luther King Jr. in Atlanta in 2004. As national IWFR Communications Director David Koff put it, "Immigrants' rights are

Photo: Paul T. Erickson/Tri-City Herald

COALITION COMMUNICATIONS

You and your allies can make beautiful music together, but to have the sort of success that the Immigrant Worker Freedom Ride enjoyed, you've all got to be singing the same song. Here are some considerations to help strengthen coalition communications and messaging:

- Goals are your glue: Be very clear about exactly what you are working together to achieve. Clarity about what is not included in the goal is also important. Manage expectations.

- Crucial messengers: Include all the voices needed to carry the message to target audiences. Every campaign demand should have a messenger to carry it, and every target audience should be able to find a credible messenger among your ranks.

- Too many cooks make for a mushy message – don't try to please every one all the time. Edit for deal-breakers, not details.

- Share strengths to build for the long term win: Encourage organizations with different skills and strengths to coach each other, offer trainings, etc. You want to strengthen your allies not just for this fight, but for the fights that lie ahead.

- Provide regular updates to talking points. Ensure that timely responses are provided when key details develop or when rapid response may be needed.

now part of the civil rights agenda." And from within the AFL-CIO, civil rights leaders like Rev. James Orange are working to ensure that recognition of the concerns of immigrant workers will be central to the organizing campaigns and political agendas of the labor movement.

According to Koff, bipartisan support has developed for the Agricultural Job Opportunity, Benefits, and Security (AgJobs) Act (S. 1645/H.R. 3142) and the DREAM /Student Adjustment Act (S. 1545/H.R.1684), which would allow undocumented students who completed high school in the U.S. to enroll in state universities as residents (which would qualify them for cheaper, in-state tuition) and to apply for legal status.

From among its 900 riders, the IWFR created a cadre of leaders trained as advocates and speakers who put a human face—the face of immigrant workers themselves – on the otherwise abstract issue of immigration. Under the rubric of a "National Call to Defend Immigrants," many of these riders are now gathering volunteers who will travel to the border areas of Arizona and to south Florida to register immigrant voters and to encourage civic participation by immigrants regardless of their status.

The cultivation of leadership and new public attitudes toward immigrants will continue through the 2004 electoral season and beyond. The pressure is on for comprehensive immigration reform.

Laura Saponara works as a consultant to nonprofits and labor unions and is a coeditor of this book. Effusive thanks to David Koff, Senior Research Analyst with the Hotel Employees and Restaurant Employees International Union and national Communications Director for the Immigrant Workers Freedom Ride.

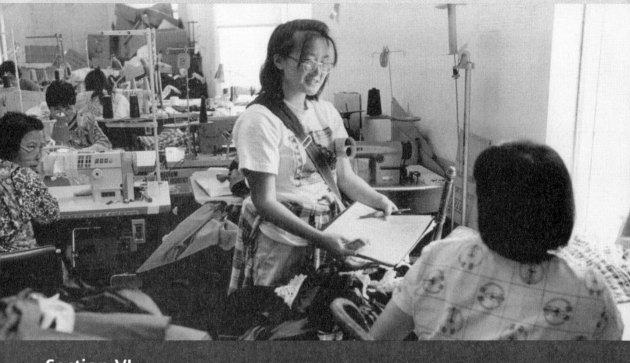

Photo: Scott Braley

Section VI

CRITICAL
CONSTITUENCIES

Every opinion counts, especially in America, where the public is divided
right down the middle on most issues. That means every person, every
audience is now crucial. These articles will help you reach out to and be
heard by people in African-American, Latino, and Lesbian, Gay, Bisexual,
and Transgender (LGBT) communities. In this section, seasoned advocates
share research and experience about how to engage young voters, and
offer encouragement and ground rules for involving religious leaders in
your election-year efforts.

Outreach to potential voters is also both encouraged by and rewarded
by funders. Here, two grant makers provide their views on the
significance of strengthening democracy by increasing the numbers
of people who make their voices heard.

Photo: Mimi Ho, a member of Californians for Justice, speaks
to seamstresses in Oakland, California, about registering to vote.

BATTLEGROUND DEMOCRACY

By Holly Minch

This election year is likely to focus intensely on 16 or 17 states that are thought to be key in the outcome of the presidential race. As in 2000, these states are likely to be won or lost by very narrow margins. Community groups in these states have an important opportunity to get press coverage of their issues. These won't be the only places you're working in 2004, but since they're in the mix, non-profits should know the rules of engagement in key states.

All politics is local, so the saying goes, and that's never more true than in these so-called battleground states. Because the presidential candidates and the national media will be focusing on these states, issue-oriented groups have the opportunity to elevate their issues from local concerns to national importance.

Recently, residents of Florida, Michigan, Tennessee, Iowa, and Wisconsin—all competitive states with industries reliant on trade with Europe—saw their local concerns move front and center on the national stage. In December 2003, the Bush administration decided to repeal tariffs on imported steel to head off a trade war in which foreign countries would have retaliated with their own tariffs against products exported from these politically important states. President Bush made the decision in spite of potential backlash in several steel-producing states of the Rust Belt—including Pennsylvania, West Virginia, and Ohio—states that have been severely hit by losses in manufacturing jobs and will be among the most closely contested in this re-election race.

This sort of electoral math will result in intense political calculation in battleground states in 2004. Here are a few do's and don'ts to guide your work in battleground states.

Do:

Make Your Issue Visible

Use the attention of hot campaigns to raise the profile of your issues, but remember that 501(c)(3)s must tread with care as activities in battleground states may draw a higher level of legal scrutiny. Your activities in these key states must not be designed to influence the outcome of the elections—only to highlight the importance of your issues.

Shape Media Coverage of the Issues

Election coverage in key states tends to offer sharper focus on issues, relying less on the typical personality politics. Local journalism will focus on key issues resonating in the campaign, while community groups can help visiting national media to connect the dots between national and local issues.

Educate Voters

The possibility for information being distorted is profound in the battleground states, where the two main-party candidates will be battling for small margins of voters. Inevitably, they'll spend huge amounts of money on broadcast advertising to reach a relatively small number of voters. This situation will be especially acute in small states like Maine, Arizona, New Mexico, Nevada, Iowa, Oregon, and in other regions where there are few independent media organizations. It will be up to local community groups to educate voters on the facts. After being bombarded by advertising messages, voters in key states are often eager to hear from local organizations—those they knew and trusted before the election started—to help them sort out the information and understand the issues. For 501(c)(3) organizations, this means distributing neutral information to voters about contested issues without mentioning candidates.

Get Out the Vote

Where the margins are narrow and media coverage of the issues intense, local groups can use the excitement and attention of the race to spur increased participation in the political process. Local charities that happen to be in battleground states like Michigan or Florida can engage in nonpartisan civic participation activities, like voter registration and Election Day mobilization. Charitable nonprofits in battleground states should focus on those civic engagement strategies that are fully permissible for 501(c)(3)s and use those strategies to engage and mobilize their communities. (See Section 3 for discussions of permissible activities.)

Don't:

Cross the Line

Issue advocacy can quickly cross the line into electioneering, especially in competitive states. For example, issue ads can be considered campaign intervention if they praise some candidates or attack others right before an election. Ads that implicitly or explicitly invite voters to cast their ballots for candidates that agree with the organization's position are not OK for 501(c)(3) organizations.

Cherry-Pick

National organizations may not realize that targeting activities to battleground states shortly before an election may cross the line if the circumstances suggest that the organizations are picking battleground states in order to influence the election. Charitable organizations cannot do GOTV or voter registration that is aimed at changing the outcome of any election. If you plan to engage in battleground states, you must have a clear logic about why, and that logic must be consistent with activities you would conduct in an off-year.

Mix Issue Advocacy and GOTV

The cautious rule for nonpartisan voter registration and GOTV is that no advocacy message should be included. Two types of GOTV messages are safe: generic, it's-a-good-thing-to-vote-type messages and references without advocacy to a broad range of issues ("civil rights, clean air and water, health care: all good reasons to vote"). GOTV should be strictly separate from issue advocacy efforts, lest the IRS think you are using them in combination to influence the outcome of the election, which is strictly off-limits for 501(c)(3) organizations.

Fly Without a Net

Because activities in battleground states can draw increased legal scrutiny, we encourage groups contemplating engagement in these states to get legal counsel.

SOUTHWEST VOTER REGISTRATION AND EDUCATION PROJECT: GIVING A LATINO VOICE TO THE VOTE

By Laura Saponara

Operating under the straightforward motto of "su voto es su voz" (your vote is your voice), the Southwest Voter Registration and Education Project (SVREP) is working to reverse the trend of under-participation by Latino voters in important elections. In Latino communities across the Southwest, SVREP is educating new voters about the democratic process. The focus is on the importance of voter registration and increasing voter participation.

"We gain power by strengthening and exercising our fundamental right to vote," says SVREP Vice President Lydia Camarillo.

SVREP has been serving communities in the Southwest for more than 20 years. The organization first opened its doors to increase statewide political and civic participation of Latinos. Since then, SVREP has conducted more than 2,200 voter registration campaigns in 14 states and successfully litigated more than 100 court cases involving voting rights. The Los Angeles office oversees a network of more than 30,000 Latino civic leaders and activists in five states who have conducted get-out-the-vote projects in more than 250 cities across the Southwest over the last 25 years.

Through the work of SVREP and other organizations, the number of Latino voters increased from 2 million in 1974 to 7.7 million in 2001. During the 1996 presidential elections, 1.3 million Latinos turned out to vote in California—a 37.5 percent increase from 1992. Latinos cast 1.61 million votes in California in the 2000 election, an increase of 268,000 votes, or 19.8 percent, over the 1996 election. Latinos also represented a record 15.2 percent of all votes cast in California in 2000.

Consequently, the number of Latino elected officials has also increased to more than 6,000 nationwide. This rise in Latino political participation can be attributed largely to community information, mobilization, and coalition-building efforts. As population growth and demographic shifts increase the sheer number of eligible Latino voters, SVREP wants to ensure that civic involvement keeps pace.

Photo: Scott Braley

SVREP is spearheading two new campaigns in 2004:

"Campaign for Communities": Mobilizing 1 Million Minority and Youth Voters:
SVREP is partnering with Earthday Network, Project Vote, and the National Association for the Advancement of Colored People (NAACP) to register 1 million minority and youth voters in eight states.

"10-4 Campaign": Raise the Latino Vote to 10 Million in 2004:
SVREP is focusing on young, low-income, and recently-registered voters in areas where Latinos and other ethnic minorities are concentrated. The goal is to mobilize 2 million new Latino voters to get to the polls during the 2004 general elections, raising the national totals to 10 million registered voters and 7.5 million votes cast.

Public education and voter registration work are underway in Arizona, California, Colorado, Florida, Georgia, Idaho, Nevada, New Mexico, North Carolina, Oregon, Oklahoma, Texas, Utah, and Washington. The timing of these activities corresponds to the electoral cycles for municipal elections, primary elections, and the general election.

"Because we work from election cycle to election cycle, we try to energize the community, build on what is exciting. The overall objective is Latino empowerment," says Camarillo.

With more than 35 million Latinos in the U.S., the hard work of strengthening democracy by inviting participation at the grassroots continues.

LATENT LATINO VOTING POWER

When considering the Latino vote, reflect on this potentially empowering statistic: There are as many unregistered Latinos who are American citizens as there were Latino voters in 2000—more than 5.5 million. These potential voters cry out for mobilization, for registration, for contact on issues they care about, for get-out-the-vote.

There are four states in particular—New Mexico, Nevada, Arizona, and Florida—where groups like SVREP can help Latino voters harness their unused voting power. In these states, large numbers of previously disengaged voters could demand an agenda that includes decent wages, retirement security, reining in corporate corruption, rebuilding public schools, labor rights, and health care.

New Mexico: In 2000, 43 percent of the state's Latinos were not registered to vote. New Mexico now has aggressive Latino Governor Bill Richardson, who is mobilizing hard to increase the power of the Latino vote nationwide.

Nevada: In 2000, 53 percent of the state's Latinos were not registered to vote.

Nevada has essentially doubled its Latino share of the population in only ten years—in 1990, Nevada was 10.4 percent Latino; by 2000, it was 19.7 percent.

Arizona: In 2000, 50 percent of the state's Latinos were not registered to vote. Arizona is already one-quarter Latino, and according to the Census, of the more than 325,000 people added to the state between April 2000 and July 2002 (the latest estimate), more than half (181,000) were Latinos.

Florida: In 2000, 36 percent of the state's Latinos were not registered to vote. The Sunshine State is now 17 percent Latino. Most Cuban Americans are already registered to vote, but thousands and thousands of non-Cuban-American Latinos are not, a fact the SVREP has recognized.

Given the explosive growth rates for Latinos in America, adding these new Latino voices and votes into the mix will transform democracy, and ensure that our political process is responsive to the values and issues that Latinos communities hold dear.

Excerpted, with permission, from "Blue States Latino Voters," by Steve Cobble and Joe Velasquez, The Nation, 1/15/04.

BLACK VOTERS MOBILIZING FOR 2004 ELECTION

By Hazel Trice Edney, National Newspaper Publishers Association

Many African Americans are still angry at how the black vote was undermined in 2000—and they want to make sure it doesn't happen again. According to the U.S. Commission on Civil Rights, nearly 200,000 votes in Florida alone were lost in that election because of faulty voting machines and ballots, voter intimidation, and confused poll workers. The commission also reported that black voters in Florida were nearly ten times more likely than non-black voters to have their ballots rejected.

Nationally, an estimated 4 million to 6 million votes were lost in 2000 because of voting foul-ups, according to the Massachusetts Institute of Technology (MIT).

A number of black organizations are working hard to see that Election 2004 provides equal representation of blacks—and that their votes are counted.

The National Coalition for Black Voter Participation (NCBVP), a nonprofit group of more than 80 organizations that encourages civic activism in the black community, is working with the nation's nine major black fraternities and sororities on a string of voter registration projects. It has also contributed to UniverSoul Circus, a traveling black production, urging audiences to register to vote and turn out at the polls. The group is also

launching Unity '04, a coalition of a dozen black organizations that will use their collective strength to implement a series of voter initiatives leading up to the November election.

The African-American Ministers Leadership Council (AAMLC), a nonpartisan arm of People for the American Way, is a group of about 100 ministers from around the country that has launched a voter registration drive in seven states. The program, called "Sanctified Seven," aims to make a strong impact in states where statewide races are normally tightly contested. The group is also paying special attention to states where the black voting-age population is large enough to mean the difference between victory and defeat. The ministers are encouraging individual parishioners to register at least seven

people every few days and, just as importantly, to get them to show up at the polls.

The following chart shows the difference
between the black voting-age population and
their turnout rates in the seven states of the
"Sanctified Seven."

In just one month, according to Rev. Romal
J. Tune of Washington, the national field
organizer for the ministers' program, the
group registered more than 2,000 new voters
in Cleveland. "People are very energized and
interested in the issues," Tune says. "Ministers'
groups and congregations have been doing
registration at malls, shopping centers, grocery stores. They do what we call 'walks
around the community' in a seven-block
radius of the church. We call them Jericho
walks, knocking on doors. And then we have
people in the pews who have influence in
their workplace. They start with registering
the entire congregation. And then the congregation goes out into other places. One
lady said, 'I went to my bowling league and I
registered 20 people.'"

The "Sanctified Seven" campaign is reminis-
cent of "Arrive with Five!," the 2000 campaign that encouraged black voters in Florida
to carry five people with them to the polls,
bolstering the black vote by 15 percent in
that state. "I think it [the 2000 election]
clearly showed the need for people—
especially African Americans—to get out
and vote, and how even a couple of thousand
votes can make a difference in the presidential election," says Cheryl Cooper, executive
director of the National Council of Negro
Women.

Cooper observes what is at stake in this election and its implications for so-called minority groups: "When you look at the potential
assaults on affirmative action and on women's
rights, and when you look at the judicial
nominees that are being put forth by this
administration, there are some real concerns
about turning back the clock, eroding some
of the significant gains that people of color
and women have made in the past decade."

*Hazel Trice Edney is the Washington Correspondent for the National Newspaper Publishers Association.
NNPA, also known as the Black Press of America, is a 62-year-old federation of more than 200 black
community newspapers from across the United States.*

Nineteen-year-old Steven Sherrier (right), who works with church community programs, helps to register voters at the intersection of Madison and Smith Streets in downtown Perth Amboy, New Jersey (2000). Photo: Eli Reed/Magnum

KNOW YOUR VOTING RIGHTS:
A GUIDE FOR VOTERS AND PEOPLE DOING VOTER REGISTRATION

By Ludovic Blain III

Registering and voting aren't as easy as they should be. We learned from Election 2000 that it isn't enough to want to vote, to show up at the polling place, or even to cast your ballot. Many people were taken off the voter rolls even though they were actually eligible; some never got to vote because polling places closed even as lines of would-be voters snaked out the door; many votes weren't counted; and some that were counted were attributed to the wrong candidate because voters were confused by the text or design of ballots.

Voters have to know their rights to make sure their vote is accurately counted. Here are a few voter tips to help reduce confusion, frustration, and disenfranchisement in 2004. Much of the information specific to your state will be available from your local board of elections, secretary of state, or the League of Women Voters.

Invariably, there will be Election Day problems, but we can try to make sure they aren't large enough to affect the election, and that real problems are documented so that we can remove remaining barriers and enable every eligible American to register and vote.

Registering

Voter Registration Forms. The Help America Vote Act (HAVA) of 2002 requires states to add new questions to their voter registration forms, including requesting a Social Security or driver's license number. People who don't fill out these sections are more likely to have to show identification at the polls.

Felon Disenfranchisement. State laws vary about whether citizens can vote after a felony conviction. Thirteen states, including Florida, Mississippi, and Washington, permanently strip the right to vote from at least some people and often require ex-felons to go through arduous processes to regain this right. Maine, Vermont, and Puerto Rico allow citizens to vote while in prison. All the other state laws fall somewhere in the middle. Make sure you know your state law; many people who are actually eligible don't know it.

Registration Deadlines and Election Day Registration. Most states have voter registration deadlines ten to 30 days before a national election. Anyone who may want to vote must be registered before the deadline. Six states allow eligible citizens to register and vote the day of the election.

Voting

Voter ID. HAVA also mandates that first-time voters registering by mail present, upon arrival at the polls, a photo ID, utility bill, or government form showing the voter's address. Get the list of acceptable IDs from your local board of elections or secretary of state and circulate it widely. It might make the difference between having a person's ballot count or not.

Provisional Ballots. HAVA also requires all states to create a backup system for voters. A person may cast a provisional ballot if their name is not on the voter list at the polls, if they don't have the necessary ID, if they're challenged by an election official, or if the polling place is closed. Some states may not count provisional ballots cast at an incorrect polling place, so the voter should ask if they are at the right polling place if their name is not on the list. If they are at the correct polling place, they should cast a provisional ballot. If they are not at the correct polling place, they should only cast a provisional ballot if they cannot get to the correct voting site.

Voting Machines. Many states have purchased new voting machines. Voters and poll workers may be confused by the new systems. Fairs or events put on by local election boards may have voting machine demonstrations where voters can try out the machines.

Voting Information. Each polling place is supposed to display a poster showing a sample ballot, instructions on how to vote and/or how to cast a provisional ballot, as well as instructions for first-time voters who may have to show ID. Even if you don't need the information, someone else might, so when you go vote, look around for the poster to make sure it is visible for other would-be voters.

Ludovic Blain III is Associate Director of the Democracy Program at Demos, a network for ideas and action. Demos is a nonpartisan public policy organization working to improve our democracy, to strengthen effective government, and to foster greater economic opportunity.

QUEER EYE FOR THE STRAIGHT VOTER

By Robert Bray

Wedding bells could dominate the 2004 elections for lesbian, gay, bisexual, and transgender (LGBT) Americans. Same-sex marriage has ascended to the level of a major political issue, with President Bush highlighting it in his 2004 State of the Union speech, the Democratic candidates carefully stepping into the fray, the social conservatives rallying their troops with it, and queers wondering if it's too early to pop the champagne and cut the cake.

Gay marriage surely is the most prominent issue in this year's elections for LGBT people. But there are other issues that activists—gay or straight—who believe in equality should be aware of. The 2004 election cycle presents the opportunity—and heightened media attention—to educate the public about pressing issues of fairness and equality for gay Americans. Following is a brief checklist of a few of the key issues likely to see increased exposure and debate this election year.

Marriage

Three recent landmark court decisions pushed this issue to the forefront: the June 2003 ruling by Ontario, Canada's high court that same-sex couples should have the right to marry; the U.S. Supreme Court ruling the following week that antigay sodomy laws violate the U.S. Constitution's right to privacy; and the November 2003 Massachusetts Supreme Judicial Court ruling that to deny marriage to same-sex couples violates that state's equal protection and due process guarantees. Then came San Francisco's decision to issue marriage licenses to same-sex couples, which touched off a firestorm of national media coverage and debate.

These events set in motion a feeding frenzy among antigay activists, mobilizing the rank and file like never before and pushing the topic right into prime time. (By the way, Boston will be the site of the Democratic Convention this year, making it a handy target for antigay forces because of the Massachusetts marriage ruling.) Religious conservatives are expected to put their faith in the preemptive federal marriage amendment to the U.S. Constitution, designed to protect the "sanctity of heterosexual marriage."

Then there is the current Administration's $1.5 billion "healthy [read straight] marriage" initiative to promote marriage, particularly among poor people, attached as a rider to the welfare reauthorization bill. The measure would spend millions on teaching low-income people the skills to enter and maintain "healthy marriages." (For an excellent analysis of the measure, visit www.alternet.org and read Traci Hukill's piece, "Who Wants to Marry a Marriage Initiative?")

"Marriage is the vocabulary and frame by which the antigay 'family' movement wants to talk about gay Americans," says Sean Cahill, director of the National Gay and Lesbian Task Force Policy Institute. "It is a hook to get people to pay attention to their analysis of what is wrong with America, and that includes homosexuality. It's designed to divide people."

Cahill notes that the federal marriage amendment to the U.S. Constitution would ban not only gay marriage but basically *any* form of family protection or recognition for gay and lesbian couples, from health insurance for domestic partners and hospital visitation rights to civil unions.

The gay marriage battle didn't just erupt spontaneously on the national political scene, despite the recent court rulings. It percolated up from the grassroots for more than a decade with statewide "Defense of Marriage" acts. More than a dozen measures banning gay marriage, in some cases through the amendment of state constitutions, are in the works. These measures, like the federal Constitutional amendment, galvanize conservative voters at the polls.

"The same groups that are making gay marriage such a wedge issue are those that oppose affirmative action and scapegoat immigrants," says Cahill. "Gay and nongay social change activists have a shared interest and a shared risk in this battle."

Adoption and LGBT Families

Equal treatment of gay and lesbian parents has not yet come up as an election issue as much as gay marriage, but activists caution that it might. "I predict this could become a campaign issue by the time the elections roll around," says NGLTF's Cahill. "Typically, attacks on gay marriage are connected to attacks on gay adoption and parenting. It's a family issue, and the Far Right wants to stake that terrain out."

HIV/AIDS Prevention and Treatment

HIV/AIDS has not made as big a splash in the current campaign as it has in previous election years, but AIDS activists say it could become more of a political factor.

Candidates may be grilled on whether they support sex education programs that stress condom use. "Abstinence-only" education campaigns have been the hallmark of the current administration, with a surge in funding for such programs and "audits" of programs and services that teach otherwise. Even the headline-making 2003 State of the Union commitment of funds to Africa to fight AIDS was couched in sex education based on abstinence-only tenets.

AIDS funding continues to be a concern. Many states are reeling from budget cuts that could disastrously affect HIV/AIDS care and prevention. For example, in California and other states, the AIDS Drug Assistance Program, which provides life-saving medications to low-income people with AIDS, is slated for serious cuts. Federal support and reauthorizations at acceptable levels are critical, so watch for AIDS activists to hound candidates on this issue along the campaign trail.

Newlyweds leave San Francisco city hall following their February 2004 wedding ceremony.   Photo: Derek Powazek

Discrimination Based on Sexual Orientation

Another issue likely to see the spotlight this year is discrimination against LGBT people. Many queer voters and their friends will be watching the candidate's positions on the Employment Non-Discrimination Act (ENDA), now in Congress.

Gays in the Military

Lifting the military ban on gays and lesbians in the Armed Forces has been a perennial political hot potato, going back to President Clinton's first presidential race in 1992. The current policy, "Don't Ask, Don't Tell," is on the books and hasn't stopped the tide of discharges of out gay and lesbian service members. As the war in Iraq drags through the election season, we may see this issue in the spotlight again.

Challenge Intolerance

Once again queers find themselves in the political crosshairs this election year. But despite the intensified attacks on gay marriage, this battle offers all social change activists—gay or not—an opportunity to challenge intolerance and bigotry. For more information on LGBT issues that may garner the spotlight in 2004, visit www.thetaskforce.org/electioncenter, on the Web site of the National Gay and Lesbian Task Force, or www.hrc.org, the Web site of the Human Rights Campaign.

Robert Bray is Founding Director and Senior Consultant at the SPIN Project, a nonprofit group of communications specialists who provide capacity-building to nonprofit public-interest organizations across the nation.

ENGAGING YOUNG VOTERS, 2004 AND BEYOND

By Twilight Greenaway

Late in 2003, the state Public Interest Research Groups launched the New Voters Project, aimed at increasing youth voter turnout in six states. Relying heavily on door-to-door canvassing—a method that has been shown to yield a consistent 8 to 10 percent increase in voter turnout—and other personal contact, the project intends to send record numbers of youth to talk with millions of their peers wherever they can find them, from the clubs to the mall.

The New Voters Project is not alone in recognizing young people as a critical constituency. In fact, there might be more nonpartisan voting messages aimed at youth this year than ever before, with dozens of groups rocking, rapping, and punking the vote.

To many of us, this is not a surprise. Both Republicans and Democrats are pouring time and resources into the groups they deem swing voters. Just as marketing professionals went into a turn-of-the-millennium frenzy over the untapped consumer power of generation Y, political consultants are all over the idea of growing a new, life-long voter base.

"Keeping it Real"

The irony is that even as they are touted as "this year's swing vote," youth are still deemed apathetic. That label may not stick. Young people may simply have a more direct approach to civic engagement. According to the 2002 report *The Civic and Political Health of the Nation: A Generational Portrait*, today's 15- to 25-year-olds are more likely to volunteer and to participate in consumer-based activism than any other generation. "Younger Americans trail their elders in attentiveness to public affairs and in electoral participation," says report researcher and George Mason University professor Scott Keeter, "but hold their own in community-related and volunteer activities and in activities that give voice to their concerns."

This desire to "keep it real" makes it tough for nonpartisan groups to engage young people in the election. The tension between speaking to issues youth care about while refraining from endorsing candidates will challenge groups working to get out the youth vote in 2004. The New Voters Project addresses this challenge by striving to treat young people as a set of individuals who care about the issues rather than like a "constituency" with a monolithic ideology.

Nonetheless, when asked which issues they are most likely to vote in response to, young people say that the war and the economy are at the top of their lists, just like they are for their parents.

Communicating Peer-to-Peer

How do we tailor our work so that it is both nonpartisan and meaningful to youth? One example can be found in the League of Independent Voters—and their Pissed Off Voters Project, led by activist and author

---

TAPPING THE YOUTH VOTE

Young people express concern over the way things are going in this country. Much like older Americans, they see terrorism, jobs and the economy, and crime as top concerns.

But how can community-based organizations reach young people to encourage them to get active? The following findings may help. They come from a 2002 nationwide survey of 2,000 18- to 24-year olds around the country, with specific attention to Asians, Latinos, and African Americans. (The survey, conducted by Lake, Snell and Perry, can be found on the Youth Vote Coalition website: www.youthvote.org/news.)

Meaning

- Most young adults would like to see better connections made between voting and the issues young adults care about.

- Young people express a desire to see how the youth vote could potentially impact the outcomes of elections where the issues that concern young adults are at stake.

Media

- A recent study from the Pew Center for People and the Press found that 20 percent of 18- to 29-year-olds regularly get news from comedy shows—like *Saturday Night Live* and *The Daily Show*—and 20 percent get their news from the Internet.

Motivation

- Drawing connections between issues young adults care about and voting is the most important way to get more young adults to vote.

Messages

- The best message for young adults is a message that focuses on the history of the vote.

- In focus groups, young people say that the message "it took 144 years for women to gain the right to vote" reaches a wide array of groups and stresses how lucky individuals are because they have the right to vote.

- A message that tells of the voting hardships that faced African Americans 40 years ago is also convincing.

Messengers

- Young adults see young politicians, other young adults, the president, MTV, and the governor of their state as the most convincing messengers to convince them to vote.

Billy Wimsatt; it's aimed primarily at young, socially engaged people who may deem themselves too progressive for electoral politics. Due out in March 2004 is the League's *How to Get Stupid White Men Out of Office,* a collection of "20 success stories from the past five years of young people who have swung or won elections." If the numbers of young progressive voters showing up to League events and visiting their Web site are any indication, they have an effective strategy: to get this generation going, remind them they're already moving.

Other well-known attempts to encourage youth voting are similarly connected with real issues. Rock the Vote added an "Issues"

20 MILLION LOUD!

Here are a few facts from the Youth Vote Coalition to counter misconceptions about the power, presence, and importance of young people in the political process:

■ Young people vote in huge numbers—almost 18 million went to the polls in 2000.

■ In almost every presidential election since 1976, more than 20 million young people ages 18 to 30 have turned out to vote on Election Day.

■ In 1996 and 2000, when that number dipped to just under 18 million, young people still made up almost 16% of the total voting population.

■ In 2000, there were more 25-year-olds who voted (1.25 million) than 75-year-olds who voted (1.07 million), and more 29-year-olds who voted (1.71 million) than 59-year-olds (1.51 million).

Source: U.S. Census, 2000

section to its Web site last year—where it provides resources on the environment, violence, and free expression, to name a few—in recognition of the fact that voting is deeply tied to people's individual political agendas. Particularly when targeting youth, it'd be a mistake not to acknowledge those agendas. For example, in choosing the name Students for an Environmentally Responsible President, one campus group wanted to communicate (nonpartisan) support of a candidate based more on the person's commitment to the environment than to a political affiliation. In this way, they acknowledge a common sentiment among young people: the idea that the Democrats and Republicans are equally removed from real-life concerns. The trick is to continue to respond to the issues that youth raise and encourage active participation and dialogue in ways that tie the issues to policy.

Organizations working to provide peer-to-peer messages can also use young people's voices to express opinions. As youth media makers have long known, giving youth the space to write personal testimonials and editorials (that are expressly not meant to represent the voice of an organization) can produce powerful messages to supplement the potentially bland, noncommittal tone youth associate with nonpartisan voting work.

The most successful nonpartisan efforts to get young people to the polls are focusing on the issues and using direct communication. This country's 24 million 18- to 24-year olds will not be reached by campaign dollars alone. Personalizing your message and providing youth with tools to speak to one another on a peer-to-peer level could mean the difference between a rerun of past election blahs or a fired-up new voter base.

Twilight Greenaway is the Project Manager for WireTap magazine, the independent information source by and for socially conscious youth. You can find it at www.wiretapmag.org.

CHURCH AND STATESMANSHIP:
INVOLVING RELIGIOUS LEADERSHIP IN POLITICAL WORK FOR SOCIAL JUSTICE

By Rev. Alexia Salvatierra

Throughout United States history, religious leaders have used their moral authority and trusted image to add credibility to struggles for civil and human rights. The role of religious leaders in the civil rights movement can't be overstated. In succeeding decades, religious leaders joined with movements opposing nuclear weapons, apartheid, and U.S. military intervention in Central America. Many activists today count on local clergy as reliable, visible voices in struggles for affordable housing and against youth violence, racial profiling, and hate crimes.

Why are faith-based messages and messengers important in an electoral year? Clergy of all denominations are in positions to encourage civic participation and to influence large numbers of congregants with messages supporting social and economic justice.

Here are some of our strengths:

- Our position as objective "third parties" without financial interest in the outcome adds credibility to social change messages.

- Our reputation as representatives of politically diverse institutions adds credibility to community coalitions that are overtly progressive.

- Our characterization of political issues as questions of justice that affect the whole community inspires community involvement.

- Direct moral, spiritual, and material support by clergy and congregants can enable community leaders to keep strong in the face of threats, intimidation, and harassment.

- We have special access to political moderates and business leaders—people who can lend key support, enhance visibility, and open doors to new constituencies.

Photo: Scott Braley

A young organizer warns a predominantly Spanish-speaking congregation in Los Angeles about Proposition 209, an anti-affirmative action measure, in advance of Election Day, 1996.

Thou Shalt Engage Clergy in 2004

Here are some suggestions to help you engage clergy in your election-year efforts:

- **Respect the time and commitments of clergy.** Urban clergy are besieged by requests for participation in community causes. They respond best to requests that make the maximum use of their time and talents. They also often have creative and strategic suggestions to offer, if allowed the opportunity.

Don't ask clergy to attend events unless they would have a role in them. Don't ask clergy to knock on doors or attend training sessions unless they'll use the training in their specific support role. Don't hide information about campaign goals or strategies.

- **Respect the requirements for religious participation.** Congregations can have complicated decision-making processes that require multiple meetings as they discuss whether to engage in political activity. Clergy sometimes face significant opposition that requires an understanding of the specific case and creative strategies to overcome. Also, be sensitive to religious holidays if you are asking religious people to participate.

■ **Offer a realistic time frame.** Don't ask for last-minute support unless you have no other alternative. Don't be inflexible about categories of participation. Sometimes it helps to identify and offer nonthreatening forms of participation that can develop a congregation's commitment gradually. For example, scheduling presentations that focus on the plight of the working poor can be an easier first involvement than presentations on voter mobilization in low-income communities.

■ **Organize religious leaders.** Don't assume that religious leaders will be automatically on board. Like anyone else, they need to be educated and encouraged to develop their capacity and commitment. Getting religious leaders together in a task force or committee that plans and implements strategies helps them to organize each other.

■ **Use the religious community's capacity to attract media.** Faith-based symbols such as ashes, bitter herbs, milk and honey, candles, and prayer vigils can create colorful events that effectively dramatize the cause.

■ **Reach out to faith-based media.** Religious media can reach voters and community members who are not necessarily reached by other media.

Lessons: Speaking the Language of Faith

In my experience with Clergy and Laity United for Economic Justice, I've seen leaders in several higher-income congregations raise issues with the campaign messages chosen by progressive nonprofit and labor organizations. These clergy have unique access to important target groups for advocacy campaigns—swing voters, political moderates, business leaders and their congregational leaders, are typically eager to volunteer to reach out to their neighbors and colleagues. However, they often find that the materials developed by (secular) social justice groups don't speak adequately to their concerns.

We have learned that clergy can have significantly greater impact on these target groups when we work with them to develop additional, alternative materials more suited to congregants of diverse socioeconomic backgrounds. For example, in the living wage campaign in Santa Monica, the core campaign message focused on the workers, but congregational leaders from higher-income congregations wanted an additional message that focused on business leaders and detailed the ways that the initiative would not hurt small business, but would rather support the economic well-being of the community. We have also found that it's worth the extra effort to design special strategies to reach people in different faith communities and denominations.

Photo: Clergy and Laity United for Economic Justice

CASE STUDY

HOW RELIGIOUS LEADERS HELPED COUNTER OPPOSITION TO A LIVING WAGE

The recent living wage campaign in Santa Monica, California, which counted on the broad and intensive involvement of religious leaders and congregations, illustrates the potential impact of the faith community.

Clergy and Laity United for Economic Justice (CLUE) became involved with the Santa Monica living wage campaign in September of 2000 after opponents launched their first major salvo—Proposition KK, a fake living wage initiative that purported to help low-wage workers but actually would have excluded luxury beach hotels from being covered by any potential living wage ordinance. Proposition KK was ultimately defeated—80 percent to 20 percent—in spite of expenditures of almost $1 million by the hotels.

- Clergy directly influenced their congregations through presentations from the pulpit and written materials. The Roman Catholic cardinal and 12 top religious authorities from different traditions signed a letter directly supporting the final living wage ordinance. Living wage activists distributed the letter in 18 local congregations the weekend before the final living wage election.

- Lay leaders formed the Worker Sanctuary Emergency Response Network to provide moral and material support to worker leaders who were suffering retaliation from their employers for their involvement in the campaign. Lay leaders participating in the Sanctuary were also called upon to volunteer for voter contact; members of 25 congregations throughout Los Angeles County participated in precinct walking or phone-banking.

Creativity in the Streets

To bring their message to the larger community, clergy and lay leaders came up with creative ways to engage the media. CLUE's "religious leaders' street theatre" events used colorful symbols, religious garb, and the shock value of agit-prop religious participation to attract media attention and to communicate a simple but memorable message.

- *"Prophets/Profits in the Marketplace"* involved ten Catholic, Protestant, Jewish and Buddhist religious leaders who stood in full vestments next to a life-size cardboard prophet at a popular outside mall and read selections from the scriptures about business leaders who defraud their workers and lie to the public. These were interspersed with workers' presentations about Measure KK's actual impact.

- In *"The Great Pie Giveaway"* 18 clergy stood at the local farmers' market under a pie chart that showed the percentage of corporate resources that would be spent on a living wage; they also gave out pieces of pie.

- In *"Bring Workers Back to the Table,"* congregation members sat down for a Thanksgiving meal at a table in the public square while workers stood around the table, with no chairs available for them to sit and eat; clergy read spiritual writings about justice.

These events were covered by local media, Hispanic/ethnic media, religious media, and some major outlets. The coverage by Hispanic media in particular helped to encourage and support workers' involvement in the campaign.

Rev. Alexia Salvatierra is Executive Director of Clergy and Laity United for Economic Justice, an interfaith association of over 400 religious leaders throughout Los Angeles County who come together to respond to the crisis of the working poor.

ETHNIC AND COMMUNITY MEDIA— USE IT OR LOSE IT

By Sandip Roy

We don't need the census to tell us that the face of America is changing rapidly. A ride on the subway in a major city like New York or San Francisco is proof enough of the demographic shifts sweeping the nation. The man absorbed in the Chinese daily, the woman reading a free bilingual Spanish weekly, the businessman flicking through a glossy Indian-American publication aimed at high-tech entrepreneurs are all part of the sea change.

These new Californians and Texans and New Yorkers are privy to a bustling, thriving world of ethnic media, a world most Americans know little about. Often relegated to second place, a sort of stepchild of American journalism, ethnic media have now become the indispensable new portal for reaching these emerging communities. In the 2004 elections, this new population has the potential to be the swing vote.

When I say "ethnic media," I mean not only giant corporations like Univisión, but also small Farsi monthlies put out in someone's living room on a desktop computer, and every mass-produced and homegrown, ethnically driven publication or broadcast in between.

Here are some facts:

- By the fall of 2019, the majority of young adults turning 18 and becoming eligible to vote in California will be Latino.

- Between 1990 and 2000, the foreign-born population grew by 200 percent or more in North Carolina, Georgia, and Nevada. The foreign-born population grew between 100 percent and 199 percent in 16 U.S. states.

- In California, Hispanic populations grew four-fold and Asian populations more than five-fold between 1970 and 1998. The population of whites increased only 11 percent over the same period.

The question is this: Does this burgeoning sector of the American population go to the ballot box? As Monica Regan and Maria Rogers Pascual document "Mobilize the Immigrant Vote" in Section 1 of this book, the answer is: not yet. In past electoral years, immigrants have not voted in proportion to their numbers. But as community-based organizations around the country speed the rate at which new immigrants enfranchise themselves, ethnic media are becoming an invaluable resource for encouraging political participation.

Reaching out to ethnic communities can make a huge difference. When Gray Davis first ran for California governor, he advertised heavily in Spanish-language media. Davis was rewarded with 78 percent of the Latino vote. During the 2003 recall, Davis chose not to advertise in Hispanic media. His vote share dropped to 53 percent. While a number of variables may have contributed to Davis's popularity drop, his declining visibi-lity in Hispanic media surely played a part.

The candidacy of ethnic community members often has the effect of mobilizing new voters, sometimes with results that may confound people who associate "diversity" with "Democrats." Though Indian Americans are generally perceived to vote for Democratic candidates, in 2003 the Indian-American community as a whole rallied behind Louisiana Republican gubernatorial candidate Bobby Jindal, who nearly became the first Indian-American governor in the nation.

The dilemma for most campaigns is how to reach this vast, growing section of the electorate. How do you get your message out to Vietnamese, Hmong, Hindi, Spanish, Russian, or Armenian speakers? These communities seem close-knit and difficult for an outsider to reach. Ethnic media can be the bridge.

For organizations trying to reach out, it's worth remembering that ethnic and community media need to be approached somewhat differently from their mainstream counterparts. Here are some pointers for tuning your message to interest ethnic media.

Think Like an Advocate

Ethnic media are media with a point of view—protecting and promoting the interests of the communities they serve. Your approach should be tailored to the concerns and interests of ethnic audiences. Remember that ethnic media's foremost role is as an advocate for ethnic communities.

For example, Chinese media were nearly alone among media in rallying to the defense of nuclear scientist Wen Ho Lee, accused of spying from his position at the Los Alamos National Laboratories. Chinese reporters showed relentless support for Dr. Lee. This helped mobilize the Chinese community to join in his defense, eventually leading to an apology from the trial judge and from former president Clinton.

Make Contact with the Community's Leadership and Local Media Mavens

Reach out to ethnic media. A personal conversation with the editor or publisher of an ethnic outlet might be all that's needed to convince a smaller paper to cover your issue in a way that reflects your message. But before you pick up the phone, do your homework. Know who the key players are. Acknowledge the leadership role of ethnic community leaders and ethnic media editors and publishers. Find ways to recognize and support ethnic media outlets, such as by having someone from your organization or campaign attend convenings or events hosted by ethnic media.

Be Issue-Based, Not Ideology-Driven

Ethnic media make ethnic people and their concerns visible. Who is the Indian scientist involved in the recent U.S. Mars expedition? How is the mad cow scare affecting the beef that's a staple of the Vietnamese noodle soup *pho*? How will the new budget affect Filipino World War II veterans' benefits? It is up to organizations trying to reach ethnic communities to frame their messages and stories for maximum relevance to the audiences.

Many nonprofits are driven by values. This is a good thing. But when reaching out to ethnic media, the translation of values to partisanship can be an instant liability. It's important to realize that ethnic media often straddle the liberal-conservative-moderate frameworks, sometimes occupying more than one at a time. Ethnic media are interested in issues as they pertain to their communities. There is opportunity in this complexity: While Vietnamese Americans may overwhelmingly support the war on Iraq and Arab Americans may be overwhelmingly against it, these communities may share convictions about many other issues, such as the rights of immigrants or the need for health care information in multiple languages.

Tailor message to dovetail with the issues of the community you want to reach. Don't assume that what's important to your organization will naturally resonate with residents of ethnic communities.

Get Specific; Avoid the "People of Color" Broad Brush

Viewing issues through a "people of color" prism may not work with ethnic media. Ethnic media may not perceive or describe ethnic community members as "people of color." Nor do editors of ethnic media assume that readers subscribe to a predetermined set of political priorities.

Be Patient; Make it Personal

Some ethnic media are run by people who hold day jobs. They may be so busy that a fax or a mass e-mail message may not be sufficient to catch their attention. Leave a message saying that you are sending the e-mail. Find out the right person to talk to and make it easy for them to be interested in reaching you. For example, an organization that advocates for immigration reform for binational lesbian or gay couples might put an Indian-American editor in contact with an Indian gay man who would be affected by this reform. Otherwise, the editor may well not think of it as an "Indian-American issue."

Make the story personal. The Patriot Act is an overwhelming topic, but discussing it in relation to the plight of Cambodian-Americans raised in the United States and being deported to Cambodia as punishment for old shoplifting incidents has immediate resonance and relevance for Southeast Asian media.

Use Ads and Forums to Drive Content

Telecommunications companies seized ethnic media in a big way in the 1990s after market research showed that ethnic consumers, often develop great brand loyalty. There is no reason your nonprofit can't or shouldn't build brand loyalty for your issue as well, so long as you abide by the constraints on political expression required for tax-exempt organizations. Consider taking out ads about your issues targeted to the paper's or station's community. (See Section 2 of this book for details on staying legal.)

Ethnic media are often shut out of mainstream media forums. Consider organizing a news briefing or debate for ethnic media about the candidates or your issue.

The Language Barrier

Don't be intimidated by the language barrier. Use a resource like New California Media's online Nationwide Ethnic Media Directory to research the media you want to approach. Don't worry that you can't speak Korean or Vietnamese. At the very least, the person who handles ads and marketing for the media outlet will most likely speak English. If you have someone on your staff who speaks the language, ask them to clue you in as to which reporter covers the beat most relevant to your issue. On the other hand, don't think that because some ethnic media outlets are in English, there's no need to make a special effort to reach out to them.

Diversifying Democracy

In many races around the country, 2004 could be the year of the ethnic voter. It's time to recognize the role ethnic media can play in communicating the issues that will compel voting. It's up to your organization to use it or lose it. As they say in the movie theaters, the audience is listening. As activists, pundits, researchers, and strategists, are we ready to talk to them?

RESOURCES FROM NCM/PACIFIC NEWS SERVICE

Our NCM directory lists the media outlets of more than 50 ethnic groups, from Afghan to Vietnamese. With 25 entries for Arizona to more than four pages of entries for New York, the directory is still just the tip of the iceberg.

New California Media's Web site, ncmonline.com, has links to the NCM online directory of ethnic media. You will also find the results of polls that identify issues of central significance to specific constituencies which can help make your case for ethnic perspectives on issue-based report. We also feature in-depth election coverage from diverse opinion leaders.

Pacific News Service (www.pacificnews.org) features commentators and analysts who will track their communities' concerns over the year. You can also tune in to our radio service for ideas about stories you may want to generate locally.

Sandip Roy is a journalist and commentator with New California Media, a nationwide association of over 700 ethnic media organizations representing the development of a more inclusive journalism.

STRAIGHT FROM THE SOURCE:
WHERE PHILANTHROPY AND POLICY MEET

We wanted to know what the philanthropic community is thinking about the 2004 elections, so we asked them directly. Included here are what two key supporters of nonprofit advocacy have to say.

The editors of *Loud and Clear* talked with **Donna F. Edwards,** Executive Director of the Arca Foundation, which has worked to curb corporate domination of U.S. politics through genuine campaign reform.

What, in your mind, is the point of intersection between philanthropy and politics?

It's not the intersection between philanthropy and politics, but the interdependence between them. So many of the critical issues that we care about as philanthropists are debated and decided through the political process. If you care about education, you have to care about politics. If you care about homelessness, you have to care about politics. If you care about foreign policy, you have to care about politics. Whether you are looking at direct service or policy change, your work depends on politics. We have to encourage the grantees that we fund to figure out the legal ways they can engage in the political process.

How would you explain the disconnect between "organizing" and engaging in electoral work?

I think the challenge is turning the organizing into allowable electoral work. It's important for grant makers who fund organizing to encourage organizers to make the links, to get people to the ballot box. The goal is to engage people who are outside of the political process to become active participants. It's an ongoing, long-term process.

There are so many nonprofits out there that do not participate in electoral activities because they are unaware they can, or are afraid of the limitations in the laws. What do you want to say to these groups?

An amazing number of resources are available that nonprofits can use to explore what the limitations are, to help them set their activities in the right legal framework. There are lawyers, advocacy organizations, and an abundance of materials that describe what groups can do to engage their communities in voter registration, issue identification, get-out-the-vote efforts, candidate forums, issue briefings, and voter guides, just to name a few non-partisan activities. It's a question of taking advantage of available resources and then seeking competent legal advice based on the specific program activities you plan to put in place.

I would also say that doing advocacy work makes you stronger, makes you relevant. It puts your allies and your detractors on notice that you are willing to fight to turn your values into public priorities. The ability to do advocacy work adds to the value of an organization.

> "Doing advocacy work makes you stronger, makes you relevant. It puts your allies and your detractors on notice that you are willing to fight to turn your values into public priorities. The ability to do advocacy work adds to the value of an organization."

Do you have any advice for groups who are seeking funding to support advocacy and elections work?

Organizations need to be strategic and focused on identifying their plans and their activities. Be careful about not taking on too much—it's better to do the smaller thing well than to fail at the larger thing. Focus is critical in this important time. Use the many resources available to make sure that your activities are within the limits allowed by law. Speak honestly with funders and the funding community about the work you intend to do.

What are the most important things nonprofits need to know going into the 2004 election cycle?

One piece of advice is that it's only a year. You can't do everything. There is a range of different kinds of organizations and entities who are doing electoral work— some of that work is appropriate for a 501(c)(3) organization and some is not. Organizations need to understand those differences so they don't get into trouble.

You've made it a point to spearhead support for a more democratic media system. How did you arrive at this priority?

Our interest in democratizing media—making sure media ownership is not concentrated in a few corporate hands—comes from our long-held interest in campaign finance reform, as well as other election reforms. We see the media as a vital component of democracy. It makes sense to fund content that elevates different voices on foreign and domestic policy. It's important to advocate for a system in which media ownership is spread broadly and not the just the property of a few companies. The nonprofit sector must play a role in shaping future media policies so that new technologies will remain open, accessible, and accountable to the public interest.

WHERE PHILANTHROPY AND POLITICS MEET
Advocacy Advisory from the Alliance for Justice

The Alliance for Justice supports a program to educate funders on the important role of nonprofit advocacy. Supporting advocacy activities is an effective way for foundations to strengthen democracy by broadening civic dialogue and giving voice to under-represented communities. By giving financial support to charities that engage in advocacy, philanthropy increases the odds of achieving its central purpose: improving the lives of ordinary Americans and communities in which they live. When grant makers and nonprofits work together, there are greater resources and opportunities for their voices to be a part of the public debate.

Public and private foundations may support nonpartisan activities. Foundations should consult their lawyers for details, but in general foundations have a great deal of flexibility in nonpartisan election-year grant-making. The key is not to fund or engage in projects that appear to support or oppose candidates for public office.

Nonprofit advocacy is a critical tool for leveraging foundation dollars on behalf of resource-thin populations, in turn benefiting disenfranchised communities and the public at large. Nonprofit organizations are known for their passion and knowledge. As a nation, we need to do a better job of tapping the expertise and insight of the researchers, service providers, and advocates in the nonprofit, independent sector. The key is for foundations to let their grantees exercise their legal right to advocate with grant funds.

We also talked with **Geri Mannion**, Chair of the Strengthening U.S. Democracy Program at the Carnegie Corporation of New York. Mannion is a veteran supporter of civic engagement programs.

How is this year different?

This is shaping up to be a very competitive election for the presidency, and that provides an opportunity to get voters (especially new or infrequent voters) excited and engaged. How often do we get an opportunity to debate and discuss our future? What does the public really want: tax cuts or a growing deficit? What would voters be willing to give up to ensure decent health care coverage for all? What do they really think about Enron— have they given up on holding these companies accountable? Do they want better environmental protections? If so, at what cost?

This year, the nation has a chance to engage in these kinds of debates. Nonprofits are often well positioned to add depth and detail to public debate.

While I have been encouraging nonprofits (and more foundations!) to get more civically engaged for years, I also encourage staff at nonprofits and foundations to get the appropriate training in conducting those activities. Training is available from such groups as Alliance for Justice and Charities Lobbying in the Public Interest.

What's your advice for groups who want to engage voters in this election?

Any nonprofit's public education and advocacy or voter engagement work should be ongoing and long-term—and, more importantly, should focus not just on the presidential or federal elections but all elections, especially local ones. Those elections are often the most neglected and it's the point

in the political process in which you are likely to engage the public more, about public schools and local tax bond issues, for example. In off-year elections, nonprofits should provide their members and constituents with information on issues they care about, should educate about whether their elected leaders are following up on promises made during the campaign, and should invite those elected leaders to meet with members should to debate issues consistently—not just during the campaign season. For example, elected leaders can come to a nonprofit's annual meeting or other community forums to meet with members who can ask them face-to-face about votes they took or positions they hold. This is especially important for poor people and young people, who don't believe their elected representatives care about them.

> "Nonprofits should provide their members and constituents with information on issues they care about and should educate about whether their elected leaders are following up on promises made during the campaign."

Nonprofits should ask their members if they are even registered to vote! This is such a simple question that many groups don't bother to ask. They ask them to write letters, to demonstrate, but often don't ask whether they vote. And they can provide links on their Web site or information in their printed materials about how to register to vote; they can also provide nonpartisan information on issues and candidates, such as through the League of Women Voters or Project Vote Smart.

Which outreach strategies seem to be effective in enhancing civic involvement and/or voter participation?

There are lots of simple things you can do to be effective. Link your Web site to nonpartisan voter registration and nonpartisan candidate information. Give voters reliable and balanced information on the issues. Help orient people to the process of voting and using the voting machine itself. It's scary for first-time voters, especially for youth and low-income people. It's like *The Wizard of Oz*: What do you do once you're behind the curtain? And this year, we'll see new voting technologies in many places. Different people approach technology differently; I have friends who are just getting used to the ATM. We need to train the current and the next generation of voters on how to use these new voting technologies and other tools.

How can nonprofits do a better job of framing the issues?

In terms of framing, many groups want to motivate people to act on the issues, but often use scare tactics. This which doesn't help inspire confidence in public leaders or the government. Use of "the sky is falling" messages can also be limiting. If the catastrophe doesn't seem to happen, the voter loses faith in these messages and the messenger.

If we want people to plug into the process of government—to believe that it's worth it to pay taxes, that voting is important and makes a difference—then we have to be able to make the case that government is worthwhile, that it has a valuable role to play in improving our communities. We need to remind people that their tax dollars are doing good for the community in the form of clean streets, public transit, safe neighborhoods, etc. We also need to educate people to understand that the government can't do it all, and choices have to be made.

Nonprofits need to remind the public that it's their government, that elected officials

work for them, and that it's up to them to oversee the way the "family" business is being run. It's the responsibility of nonprofits to connect people to the information and skills they need to run the family business!

With regard to the work of diversifying participation in our democracy, how can we measure success over time? What does success look like?

Increased voter turnout is one way to measure success. The way campaigns are financed tends to make a big difference in the number of people who vote. If you look at states like Maine and Arizona, where candidates can qualify for public financing of their campaigns at the state level, voter turnout has increased considerably. Public financing also increases the diversity of candidates; voters see people who look like them running for office because public financing makes those races affordable. And you see more parties represented, a broader range of views. Finally, you see more community involvement because people begin to feel like they can actually make a difference.

There are other ways to measure success, like fair redistricting to ensure competitive elections. In 2004, only about 30 congressional elections are expected to be competitive. No one wants to run, or bother to vote, in entrenched districts where the outcome is a forgone conclusion before the campaigns even start.

We can also measure success by the removal of structural barriers to voting, like those addressed in the Help America Vote Act, and by efforts to ensure that we have no more Floridas! Nonprofits should be involved in ensuring that HAVA is implemented well this year, especially at the local or state level.

> "Nonprofits should stop being afraid to be politically engaged. They should know the laws and the rules, and take the lead in helping to make our citizens more educated about issues."

Any advice for groups who want to sustain this advocacy work through the election year and beyond?

All nonprofits should fill out the 501(h) election form. Under 501(h), a charity may use up to 20 percent of the first $500,000 of its exempt purpose expenditures to lobby. For organizations with larger budgets, this dollar amount increases, on a sliding scale, to a maximum of $1 million. It's a simple step, and it gives clear definitions of various kinds of lobbying communications that are allowed.

In sum, nonprofits should stop being afraid to be politically engaged. They should know the laws and the rules, and take the lead in helping to make our citizens more educated about issues and candidates and more engaged in the political process. This will make our democracy more vibrant and our government more effective and accountable.

RESOURCES

POLITICAL JARGON
From the Western Progressive Leadership Network

BALLOT Paper or other form prepared by Elections officers and used by registered voters to cast their votes.

BALLOT MEASURE Another term for an initiative or referendum.

BCRA Bipartisan Campaign Reform Act (also known as McCain-Feingold). This law, passed in 2002, sets new campaign finance rules for federal elections.

DISTRICT The area represented by a public official; districts overlap for different levels of government.

GENERAL ELECTION An election where opposing candidates may represent different political parties.

HAVA Help America Vote Act. This 2001 law requires more proof of ID and will centralize voter lists statewide. Look for changes in state requirements.

INDEPENDENT A voter not affiliated with any political party.

INITIATIVE In some states, voters can sign petitions to place a certain question on the ballot in order to change or create laws.

LEGISLATION/BILL A proposed change in public law that will be debated and voted on by a legislative body.

LOBBY To support or oppose a bill or proposal for action by a legislature or other public body.

MOTOR-VOTER Method now used in many states to allow voters to register at the same time they receive a driver's license.

NONPARTISAN ELECTION An election without political party primary elections. Many city and town elections are nonpartisan, and all candidates run on one ballot.

PARTISAN ELECTION An election with candidates representing a political party. Legislative elections are usually partisan.

POLITICAL PARTY An organization in which the members share common political views (e.g., Democratic, Republican, Green).

PRECINCT The registrar of voters organizes voter lists according to precincts, often a neighborhood with a single polling place.

PRIMARY ELECTION An election within a political party to choose a candidate to run in the general election.

RE-ENFRANCHISEMENT The term for restoring the rights of citizenship (including voting rights) to people who have been convicted of felonies. Re-enfranchisement occurs after felons complete their sentences. The rules of felon re-enfranchisement vary by state.

REFERENDUM In some states, referendums enable voters to overturn laws enacted by the legislature.

REGISTERED VOTER A person who meets the legal qualifications to vote and has signed a form placing her or his name on the voter list.

REGISTRAR OF VOTERS Government officer, at county or state level, who is responsible for maintaining voting lists and conducting elections.

RUN-OFF ELECTION In nonpartisan elections, if no candidate gets more than 50% of the vote, a run-off election is often held to allow voters to choose from the top two candidates.

SECRETARY OF STATE Usually an elected official charged, among other duties, with overseeing voting practices and procedures. Most secretaries of state have Web sites with filing deadlines and other info about elections.

SLATE In some areas, candidates from the same party, or nonpartisan candidates sharing similar views, campaign as a group; this group is called the slate.

TERM OF OFFICE The number of years a political office-holder serves. The president has a four-year term, and members of the House of Representatives serve for two years.

RESOURCES FOR EFFECTIVE MEDIA STRATEGIZING ABOUT THE ELECTION

This section can help activists sharpen their awareness of available resources, increase their knowledge of the issues through suggested readings, and become more familiar with various organizations and companies that might be useful.

The section is arranged in the following manner:

1. Contributors to this kit

2. Experts on nonprofit advocacy

3. Election-related groups

4. PR/media consultants

5. Media sources

6. News services

7. Public opinion research

8. Radio actualities

9. Clipping services

10. Press release distribution services

11. Books, publications, and Web sites

12. Groups concerned with media literacy and media bias

1. Contributors

All organizations involved in this project are listed below.

Accountability Campaign
55 Washington Sq. S
New York, NY 10012
212-477-0351
www.accountabilityny.org

Advocacy Inc.
2001 S St. NW, Ste. 630
Washington, DC 20009
www.advocacyinc.com

Alliance for Justice
11 Dupont Circle NW, 2nd Fl.
Washington, DC 20036
202-822-6070
www.afj.org

AlterNet.org
77 Federal St.
San Francisco, CA 94107
415-284-1420
www.alternet.org

Apollo Alliance
c/o Institute for America's Future
1025 Connecticut Ave., Ste. 205
Washington, DC 20036
202-955-5665
www.apolloalliance.org

Arca Foundation
1308 19th St., NW
Washington, DC 20009
202-822-9193
www.arcafoundation.org

Asian Pacific American Agenda Coalition
P.O. Box 448
Boston, MA 02134
617-426-5313
www.apaac.org

Association of Community Organizations for Reform Now! (ACORN)
739 8th St. SE
Washington, DC 20003
202-547-2500
www.acorn.org

Ballot Initiative Strategy Center
1025 Connecticut Ave. NW, Ste. 205
Washington, DC 20036
202-223-2373
www.ballot.org

Brennan Center for Justice at NYU School of Law
161 Avenue of the Americas, 12th Fl.
New York, NY 10013
212-998-6730
www.brennancenter.org

California Immigrant Welfare Collaborative
926 J Street, Suite 701
Sacramento, CA 95814
916-448-6762
www.nilc.org/ciwc

Carnegie Corporation of New York
437 Madison Ave.,
New York, NY 10022
212-371-32001
www.carnegie.org

Carol/Trevelyan Strategy Group (CTSG)
1718 Connecticut Ave. NW, 6th Fl.
Washington, DC 20009
202-448-5200
www.ctsg.com

Clergy and Laity United for Economic Justice (CLUE)
548 S. Spring St., Ste. 616
Los Angeles, CA 90013
213-239-6770
www.cluela.org

Demos: A Network for Ideas & Action
220 Fifth Ave. 5th Fl.
New York, NY 10001
212-633-1405
www.demos-usa.org

Immigrant Worker Freedom Ride
www.iwfr.org

In These Times
2040 Milwaukee Ave.
Chicago, IL 60647
773-772-0100
www.inthesetimes.com

Iowa Citizens' Action Network (ICAN)
3520 Beaver Ave., Ste. E
Des Moines, IA 50310
515-277-5077
www.yawp.com/ican

Liberty Hill Foundation
2121 Cloverfield Blvd., Ste. 113
Santa Monica, CA 90404
310-453-3611
www.libertyhill.org

MoveOn
www.moveon.org

The Nation
33 Irving Pl.
New York, NY 10003
212-209-5400
www.thenation.com

**National Gay and Lesbian
Task Force**
1325 Massachusetts Ave. NW, Ste.
600
Washington, DC 20005
202-393-5177
Tty: 202-393-2284
www.ngltf.org/pi

**National Newspaper Publishers
Association**
3200 13th St. NW
Washington, DC 20010
202-588-8764
www.nnpa.org

New California Media
660 Market St., Ste. 210
San Francisco, CA 94194
415-730-5610, 925-377-6397
www.news.ncmonline.com

New Hampshire Citizen's Alliance
4 Park St., Ste. 403
Concord, NH 03301
603-225-2097
www.nhcitizensalliance.org

**Northern California
Citizenship Project**
160 14th St.
San Francisco, CA 94103
415-621-4808
www.immigrantvoice.org

Pacific News Service
275 9th St.
San Francisco, CA 94103
415-503-4170
news.pacificnews.org

Project Vote
793 8th St. SE, Ste. 202
Washington, DC 20003
800-546-8683
www.projectvote.org

Rockridge Institute
3871 Piedmont Ave., Ste. 35
Oakland, CA 94611
510-450-4835

Sierra Club
85 Second St.
San Francisco, CA 94105
415-977-5500
www.sierraclub.org

The SmartMeme Project
415-722-1846
www.smartmeme.com

**Southwest Voter Registration
Education Project**
Kelly USA Bldg. 1670
206 Lombard St., 2nd Floor
San Antonio, TX 78226
210-922-0225
www.svrep.org

UNITE!
275 Seventh Ave.
New York, NY 10001
212-265-7000
www.uniteunion.org

**Western Progressive
Leadership Network**
Western States Center
P.O. Box 40305
Portland, OR 97240
503-228-8866
www.westernstatescenter.org

WireTap Magazine
77 Federal St.
San Francisco, CA 94107
415-284-1420 ext. 328
www.wiretapmag.org

2. Experts on nonprofit advocacy

These are a few groups that can help you with the brass tack legal questions you may have about your election-related work.

Alliance for Justice
11 Dupont Circle NW, 2nd Fl.
Washington, DC 20036
202-822-6070
Nonprofit Advocacy:
www.afj.org/nonprofit

Californians for Justice
1611 Telegraph Ave., Ste. 1550
Oakland, CA 94612
510-452-2728
www.caljustice.org

Center for Community Change
1000 Wisconsin Ave. NW
Washington, DC 20007
202-342-0519
www.communitychange.org

**Charity Lobbying in the
Public Interest**
2040 S St. NW
Washington, DC 20009
202-387-5048
www.clpi.org

OMB Watch
1742 Connecticut Ave. NW
Washington, DC 20009
202-234-8494

3. Election-related groups

The groups below may be good resources for your work. Note: This list is by no means exhaustive, as there are hundreds if not thousands of organizations large and small working on election-related issues in 2004. We tried to identify groups that were national in scope so as to be relevant to all readers. We sincerely apologize for any glaring omissions in this list.

501(c)(3) Organizations

Campaign for America's Future
1025 Connecticut Ave. NW
Ste. 205
Washington, DC 20036
202-955-5665
www.ourfuture.org

Earth Day Network
1616 P St. NW, Ste. 200
Washington, DC 20036
202-518-0044
www.earthday.net

Engage America
600 Townsend St., Ste. 410W
San Francisco, CA 94103
415-865-2775
www.engageamerica.org

Industrial Areas Foundation
1244 NE 39th Ave.
Portland, OR 97232-1905
503-235-6474

Jobs With Justice
501 Third St. NW
Washington, DC 20001
202-434-1106
www.jwj.org

National Association for the Advancement of Colored People (NAACP)
4805 Mt. Hope Dr.
Baltimore, MD 21215
877-NAACP-98
www.naacp.org
For information on voter registration, voting rights, and get-out-the-vote efforts specific to your state, get in touch with your local chapter.

National Voice
2105 First Ave. S.
Minneapolis, MN 55404
886-428-7228
612-879-7500
www.nationalvoice.org

New Voters Project
1533 Market St., 2nd Fl.
Denver, CO 80202
303-573-5885
www.newvotersproject.org

Planned Parenthood Federation of America
1780 Massachussetts Ave. NW
Washington, DC 20036
202-785-3351
www.plannedparenthood.org

Project Democracy
c/o League of Conservation Voters
Education Fund
1920 L St. NW, Ste. 800
Washington, DC 20036
202-875-8683
www.lcveducation.org/news/news-main.cfm

Project Vote
793 8th St. SE, Ste. 202
Washington, DC 20003
800-546-8683
www.projectvote.org

Rock the Vote
1460 4th St., Ste. 200
Santa Monica, CA 90401
310-656-2464
www.rockthevote.com

US ACTION
1341 G St. NW, 10th Fl.
Washington, DC 20005
202-624-1730
www.usaction.org

Youth Vote Coalition
1010 Vermont Ave. NW, Ste. 715
Washington, DC 20005
202-783-4751
www.youthvote.org

501(c)(4) Organizations

Association of Community Organizations for Reform Now! (ACORN)
739 8th St. SE
Washington, DC 20003
202-547-2500
www.acorn.org

American Civil Liberties Union (ACLU)
125 Broad St., 18th Fl.
New York, NY 10004
www.aclu.org
ACLU also has a 501(c)(3) foundation. For information on voter registration, voting rights, and get-out-the-vote efforts specific to your state, get in touch with your local chapter.

League of Conservation Voters
1920 L St. NW, Ste. 800
Washington, DC 20036
202-785-8683
www.lcv.org
The League of Conservation Education Fund is a 501(c)(3) organization.

League of Independent Voters
226 W. 135th St., 4th Fl.
New York, NY 10030
212-283-8879
www.indyvoter.org

League of Women Voters
1730 M St. NW, Ste. 1000
Washington, DC 20036-4508
202-429-1965
www.lwv.org
For information on voter registration, voting rights, and get-out-the-vote efforts specific to your state, get in touch with your local chapter.

MoveOn
www.moveon.org

National Abortion and Reproductive Rights Action League (NARAL)
1156 15th St., Ste. 700
Washington, DC 20005
202-973-3000
www.prochoiceamerica.org
NARAL also has a 501(c)(3) foundation and a PAC.

People for the American Way
2000 M St. NW, Ste. 400
Washington, DC 20036
202-467-4999
www.pfaw.org
PFAW also has a 501(c)(3) foundation. Check out PFAW's Election Protection project to ensure that every eligible voter casts a ballot that counts on Election Day:
www.pfaw.org/pfaw/general/default.aspx?oid=12711

Sierra Club
85 2nd St.
San Francisco, CA 94105
415-977-5500
www.sierraclub.org

U.S. Public Interest Research Group (U.S. PIRG)
218 D St. S.E.
Washington, DC 20003
202-546-9707
www.pirg.org

Privately Held Corporations

Working for Change/ Working Assets
101 Market St., Ste. 700
San Francisco, CA 94105-1530
415-369-2000
www.workingassets.com
www.workingforchange.com
WorkingforChange.com has an online voter registration campaign.

4. PR/media consultants

You may want to pursue the use of outside PR help when working on an intensive media campaign. Here is a comprehensive list of groups that service nonprofit organizations working on social change issues. It is important to realize that some of these listings have a more national than local scope. Fenton Communications is a New York City-based outfit with a large staff; Kent Communications, on the other hand, is basically a one-person operation. Whenever considering working with PR consultants, conduct background research and make sure that the group is suitable for your organization. Look at their client lists. Talk to people on staff (note: the names listed here are the principle contacts, such as presidents or executive directors). You shouldn't have a problem finding someone who can meet your needs (and budget, too!).

Please note that the SPIN Project does not officially endorse these companies.

Bedrock Strategies, Inc.
8033 Sunset Blvd., Ste. 960
Los Angeles, CA 90046
323-962-3938

Cause Communications
Jason Salzman
1836 Blake, Ste. 100A
Denver, CO 80202
303-292-1524
newsmush@netone.com
www.causecommunications.org

Communications Consortium
Media Center
Kathy Bonk, Emily Tynes
1200 New York Ave. NW, Ste. 300
Washington, DC 20005
202-326-8700
info@ccmc.org
www.ccmc.org

Esopus Creek Communications
Jane Wholey, Charles Winfrey
1011 Orleans St.
New Orleans, LA 70116
504-528-9871
esopus@bellsouth.net

Fenton Communications
David Fenton
260 Fifth Ave.
New York, NY 10001
212-584-5000
fenton@fenton.com
www.fenton.com

Jeff Gillenkirk
415-550-0869
jeff@yourmessage.org
www.YourMessage.org

McKinney & Associates
Gwen McKinney
1612 K St. NW, Ste. 904
Washington, DC 20006
202-833-9771
marketing@mckpr.com
www.mckpr.com

The Mainstream Media Project
Mark Sommer
854 Ninth St., Ste. B
Arcata, CA 95521
707-826-9111
info@mainstream-media.net
www.mainstream-media.net

MessageWorks
Dan Newman, Principal
415-552-8495
dan@messageworks.org
www.messageworks.org

Miriam Zoll Communications
Miriam Zoll
101 Perry Street, Suite G
New York, NY 10014
917-691-2507
Miriam@zollgroup.com

ProMedia Public Relations
Robyn Stein
250 W. 57th St., Ste. 820
New York, NY 10019
212-245-0510
ProMediaNY@aol.com

Public Interest Media Group
Andrea Miller, Susan Lamontaigne
611 Broadway, Ste. 730
New York, NY 10012
212-260-1520
info@publicinterestmedia.com
www.publicinterestmedia.com

Public Media Center
Herbert Chao Gunther
466 Green St.
San Francisco, CA 94133
415-434-1403
info@publicmediacenter.org
www.publicmediacenter.org

Riptide Communications
David Lerner
666 Broadway, Ste. 444
New York, NY 10012
212-260-5000
info@riptideonline.com
www.riptideonline.com

Spitfire Strategies
Kristen Grimm Wolf
1500 21st St. NW
Washington, DC 20036
202-293-6200
www.spitfirestrategies.com

Valerie Denney Communications
Valerie Denney
407 S. Dearborn, Ste. 1175
Chicago, IL 60605
312-408-2580
info@vdcom.com
www.vdcom.com

5. Media sources

Several companies or journalist organizations help compile media directories that can provide you with a wealth of contacts to reporters and editors. The following groups offer directories that are quite diverse, both in terms of cost and/or content. For example, many of the ethnic journalist organizations' media directories are low-cost or free, provide listings of both mainstream and community ethnic press, and offer information on how to contact ethnic reporters and editors at regular mainstream outlets. The more commercial services, such as News Media Yellow Book and Bacon's, are the grand-daddies of media directories, offering comprehensive mainstream (not too many small or ethnic press are listed here) and extremely expensive media lists, available in a variety of formats. Both Bacon's and News Media Yellow Book may be found at your local library. Use these directories to augment your media databases whenever possible.

Asian-American Journalists Association
Member organizations directory
1182 Market St., Ste. 320
San Francisco, CA 94102
415-346-2051
national@aaja.org
www.aaja.org
For $50.00 you can receive listings of over 200 Asian-American-owned print and broadcast media in the U.S. on mailing labels for one-time use.

Bacon's Media Directories
332 S. Michigan Ave.
Chicago, IL 60604-4434
800-621-0561, 312-922-2400
www.bacons.com
A two-volume media directory for newspapers, magazines, radio, and TV/cable; updated and augmented quarterly. Available in hard copy ($375/vol.) or CD-ROM ($2,395/year); generally large public libraries and universities carry the hard copy for public reference.

Hispanic Yearbook
c/o TIYM Publishing Co., Inc.
6718 Whittier Ave., Ste. 130
McLean, VA 22101
703-734-1632
tiym@aol.com
www.tiym.com/
This annually updated and augmented resource directory contains well over 2,000 Hispanic-owned media listings in the U.S., categorized by media (print, radio, and TV). The National Association of Hispanic Journalists at 202-662-7145 distributes surplus (but current) copies for free. Otherwise, send a check or money order for $19.95, payable to TIYM Publishing Co., Inc. There is no additional fee for shipping and handling.

National Association of Black Owned Broadcasters
Member stations directory
1155 Connecticut Ave. NW, Ste. 600
Washington, DC 20036
202-463-8970
info@nabob.org
www.nabob.org
A nationwide directory booklet of more than 180 black-owned TV/radio stations; $25.00 fee includes shipping. Each entry includes station owner and manager names, station code, and contact information. Fax order on letterhead.

Native American Journalists Association
Member organizations directory
555 N Dakota St.
Vermillion, SD 57069
605-677-5282
info@naja.com
www.naja.com
More than 200 print and broadcast media listings in the U.S. can be obtained in hard copy or disc format for $125.00. There is no shipping and handling fee. Order by mail by enclosing a check or money order, or fax request on letterhead; specify format desired.

National Gay and Lesbian Task Force
Queer media list
1325 Massachusetts Ave. NW
Ste. 600
Washington, DC 20005
202-393-5177
ngltf@ngltf.org
www.ngltf.org
The National Gay and Lesbian Task Force regularly maintains a list of most queer media throughout the United States. Contact the group directly to find out more information.

National Newspapers Publishers Association
Member organizations directory
3200 13th St., NW
Washington, DC 20010
202-588-8764
nnpadc@nnpa.org
www.nnpa.org.
A directory of over 300 black-owned newspapers in the U.S. is available by either check or money order for $50.00, made payable to NNPA. There is no shipping and handling fee.

News Media Yellow Book
c/o Leadership Directory, Inc.
104 5th Ave., 2nd Fl.
New York, NY 10011
212-627-4140
www.leadershipdirectories.com
A national news media directory, the Yellow Book includes listings of news services, newspapers, networks, TV/radio stations, programs, periodicals, international media, and so on; updated and augmented quarterly. The hard copy subscription costs $356/year, the CD-ROM version is $2,479/year, and the Internet subscription costs $3,306. The Internet and CD-ROM versions provide the entire Leadership Directory, consisting of not only news media but also government affairs, corporate, judicial and financial yellow pages, among others; the Internet version is updated daily. There is no shipping charge for domestic orders. Most libraries and universities should carry current editions in hard copy. To order, visit the website.

6. News services

News services are a great way to cause an echo effect with the news story you're trying to get out in the public. A news service is a syndication service that supplies multiple media outlets with the same story. In this section, commercial, mainstream services, such as Associated Press, United Press International, and Reuters, have been grouped with more specialized or non-mainstream services. AlterNet.org, for example, syndicates stories by independent and alternative journalists on a wire that services more than 150 alternative and independent weeklies across the nation. Pacific News Service also has an alternative bent but places its commentary mostly in print dailies. American Forum has a very specific purpose of syndicating opinion editorials or public service announcements to print and broadcast media mainly in the South. Use this list with a keen eye, and make sure you investigate exactly what type of service is being offered. Contact your local AP, Reuters or UPI office, typically located in the nearest major city.

AlterNet.org
77 Federal St., 2nd Fl.
San Francisco, CA 94107
415-284-1420
info@alternet.org
www.alternet.org
Produces a public interest Web site offering news, features, online community, and activism opportunities; and sells content to hundreds of newspapers, Web sites, and newsletters.

American Forum
1071 National Press Building
Washington, DC 20045
202-638-1431
forum@mediaforum.org
www.mediaforum.org
Distributes opinion editorials and public service announcements to mostly Southern media.

Associated Press
National News Desk
50 Rockefeller Plaza
New York, NY 10020
212-621-1500
feedback@ap.org
www.ap.org

The Mainstream Media Project
Mark Sommer
854 Ninth St., Ste. B
Arcata, CA 95521
707-826-9111
info@mainstream-media.net
www.mainstream-media.net

Pacific News Service
275 9th St.
San Francisco, CA 94103
415-503-4170
pacificnews@pacificnews.org
www.pacificnews.org
Syndicates articles on the wire to more than 100 subscribing publications every weekday and sends out news alerts to news editors.

The Progressive Media Project
409 E. Main St.
Madison, WI 53703
608-257-4626
pmproj@progressive.org
www.progressive.org/mediaproj.htm
Solicits, edits, and distributes commentary pieces to some big, but mostly small-town newspapers.

Public News Service
(formerly Creative Communications)
Main/Outreach Office:
1810 W. State St., Ste. 420
Boise, ID 83702
208-441-1010
creative@rmci.net
www.publicnewsservice.org

PNS Boulder Office:
Lark Corbeil, Managing Editor
415 Quail Circle
Boulder, CO 80304
303-448-9105;
lark@rmci.net
www.publicnewsservice.org
Public News Service manages a multistate network of independent state news services.

PNS Onda Latina Office:
Spanish Radio Service for the
Pacific Northwest
315 Stampede Dr.
Nampa, ID 83687
Contact: Alice Mondragón Whitney
208-442-0823 ext. 112
ccispanish@rmci.net

Reuters—National News Desk
199 Water St.
New York, NY 10038
212-859-1400
editor.reuters@reuters.com
www.reuters.com

United Press International
National News Desk
1510 H St. NW
Washington, DC 20005
202-898-8000
feedback@upi.com
www.upi.com

7. Public opinion research

Public opinion research is something your organization or coalition might consider to help highlight your issues in the press. Below are a variety of companies that often work in the nonprofit social change arena.

Charlton Research Company
611 Pennsylvania Ave. SE, Ste. 408
Washington, DC 20003
202-546-1222
www.charltonresearch.com

EDK Associates, Inc.
245 E 21st St., 6th Fl.
New York, NY 10010
646-602-8818
edkpoll@aol.com

Jeffrey Pollock, President
Global Strategy Group, Inc.
895 Broadway, 5th Fl.
New York, NY 10003
212-260-8813
mail@globalstrategygroup.com
www.globalstrategygroup.com

Goodwin Simon Strategic Research
10951 W. Pico Blvd., Ste. 329
Los Angeles, CA 90064
310-446-7752

San Francisco Office:
870 Market St., Ste. 1074
San Francisco, CA 94102
415-835-9889
info@goodwinsimon.com
www.goodwinsimon.com

Greenberg Quinlan Rosner Research Inc.
10 G St., NE Ste. 400
Washington, DC 20002
202-478-8330
www.greenbergresearch.com

Lake, Snell, Perry & Associates
1726 M St. NW Ste. 500
Washington, DC 20036
202-776-9066
info@lspa.com
www.lakesnellperry.com

Peter Hart Research Associates
1724 Connecticut Ave. NW
Washington, DC 20009
202-234-5570
info@hartresearch.com
www.hartresearch.com

RIVA (Research in Values & Attitudes)
7316 Wisconsin Ave., Ste. 450
Bethesda, MD 20814
301-652-3632
research@rivainc.com
www.rivainc.com

8. Radio actualities

Anyone can produce a radio actuality at a reasonable price. However, if you're looking for help, the group listed below can help you with production and distribution at a reasonable price.

The January Group
1515 Jefferson Davis Hwy., Ste. 1220
Arlington, VA 22202
703-418-2060

National Radio Project
1876 16th Ave.
San Francisco, CA 94122
415-665-6764

9. Clipping services

Clipping services are designed to help you keep track of your press coverage or press coverage of an issue in which you are interested, by relieving you of the responsibility of following your story in the papers, on TV, over the radio, and otherwise. Some clipping services are extremely expensive, and thus cost-prohibitive. Recently, free services have surfaced with the onset of Internet communications, such as Excite.com. Shoppers beware! Some services may cost more than others.

Allen's Press Clipping Bureau
657 Mission St., Ste. 602
San Francisco, CA 94105
415-392-2353

Bacon's Clipping Bureau
Bacon's Information Inc.
332 S. Michigan Ave.
Chicago, IL 60604
800-621-0561, 312-922-2400
www.bacons.com
Reads general- and special-interest publications nationwide, including wire services, with the exception of the smallest rural papers. In addition, broadcast transcripts and Internet monitoring are available.

Burrelle's/Luce Press Clippings
75 East Northfield Rd.
Livingston, NJ 07039
800-631-1160, 973-992-7675
moreinfo@burrellsluce.com
www.burrellsluce.com
Reads and covers both print and broadcast media. TV/radio transcript services are designed to complement print clipping service.

Delahaye Medialink Worldwide
800 Connecticut Ave., 1st Fl.
Norwalk, CT 06854
800-227-7409
sales@delahayemedialink.com
www. delahayemedialink.com
Offers tracking reports, video clips, air checks and news transcripts from TV stations around the country and abroad.

Lexis-Nexis Group
P.O. Box 933
Dayton, OH 45401
800-227-9597
www.lexis.com
Lexis-Nexis provide a search engine for print media and public records.

Video Monitoring Services of America
330 W. 42nd St. 29th Fl.
New York, NY 10036
212-736-2010
nyassales@vidmon.com
www.vidmon.com
Tracks coverage ranging from segments to commercials on both radio and TV, and in print media nationwide.

webclipping.com
A division of AllResearch, Inc.
8217 Beverly Blvd., Ste. 6
Los Angeles, CA 90048
info@allresearch.com
www.webclipping.com
Searches over 30 of the largest engines on the World Wide Web and all of the Usenet discussion groups as well as electronic publications.

10. Press release distribution services

These services will distribute your press release to journalists to augment your media exposure, as well as decrease your workload in getting out your press release.

Ascribe Newswire
5464 College Ave., Ste. B
Oakland, CA 94618
510-653-9400
info@ascribe.org
www.ascribe.org
Transmits news releases via the Associated Press. Known as "the public interest newswire," Ascribe also feeds news to major news retrieval database services, online publications, developers of Web sites and intranets.

PR News Wire
888-776-0942
information@prnewswire.com
www.prnewswire.com
Broadcast faxes your press release to their media contact base, or to one you provide.

US Newswire
National Press Bldg., Ste. 1230
Washington, DC 20045
202-347-2770, 800-544-8995
info@usnewswire.com
www.usnewswire.com

11. Books, publications, and Web sites

The following publications will help you to better understand how the media system works both for and against you. Topics range from proactive media strategizing to grappling with media bias, and messages are aimed at both traditional activists and media activists as well. Where titles are self-published by activist organizations, the contact information for them is listed.

The Activist Cookbook: Creative Actions for a Fair Economy. Andrew Boyd. United for a Fair Economy: Boston, MA, 1997.
To obtain a copy, contact:
United for a Fair Economy
37 Temple Pl., 2nd Fl.
Boston, MA 02111
617-423-2148
research@faireconomy.org
www.faireconomy.org

FAIR's Media Activism Kit. FAIR, New York, NY: 1998.
To obtain a copy, contact:
Fairness and Accuracy in Reporting (FAIR)
112 West 27th St.
New York, NY, 10001
212-633-6700
212-727-7668
fair@fair.org
www.fair.org

We the Media: A Citizen's Guide for Fighting for Media Democracy. Don Hazen and Julie Winokur. The New Press: New York, NY, 1997.
To obtain a copy, contact:
Independent Media Institute
77 Federal St.
San Francisco, CA 94107
415-284-1420
info@independentmedia.org
www.independentmedia.org

Strategic Communication for Nonprofits. Larry Kirkman and Karen Menichelli, eds. The Benton Foundation: Washington, D.C., 1992.
To obtain a copy, contact:
The Benton Foundation
1625 K St. NW, 11th Fl.
Washington, DC 20006
202-638-5770
benton@benton.org

Public Opinion Polling: A Handbook for Public Interest and Citizen Advocacy Groups. Celinda C. Lake. Island Press: Washington, D.C., 1987.

Making Radio Work for You. Families USA Foundation: Washington, D.C., 1996.
To obtain a copy, go online to:
http://www.familiesusa.org/site/PageServer?pagename=Publications_Radio_Guide
Or contact:
Families USA Foundation
1334 G St., NW
Washington, DC 20005
202-628-3030
info@familiesusa.org
www.familiesusa.org

Making the News. Jason Salzman. Westview Press: Boulder, CO, 2003.

Media Advocacy and Public Health. Lawrence Wallack, et al. Sage Publications: Thousand Oaks, CA, 1993.

The Publicity Handbook. David R. Yale. NTC Business Books: Lincolnwook, IL, 1991.

PR Web
P.O. Box 333
Ferndale, WA 98248
360-312-0892
www.prweb.com
In addition to providing a free database to post press releases, this site lists many PR resources and links.

Prime Time Activism. Charlotte Ryan. South End Press: Boston, Massachusetts, 1991.

How to Tell and Sell Your Story. Timothy Saasta. Center for Community Change: Washington, D.C., 1997.
To obtain a copy, contact:
Center for Community Change
1000 Wisconsin Ave. NW
Washington, DC 20007
202-342-0519
info@communitychange.org
www.communitychange.org

SPIN Project Web site
www.spinproject.org/spin
Provides media resources, tips and tools.

SPIN Works! A Media Guidebook for the Rest of Us. Robert Bray: 2002.
To obtain a copy, contact:
www.spinproject.org/resources/order.php3
or call: 415-284-1420, ext. 309

12. Groups concerned with media bias and media literacy

The groups listed below seek to expose how mainstream media often mis- or under-represents various groups and/or issues due to ethnic, gender, class, or sexual orientation biases. In some cases, organizations such as Fairness and Accuracy in Reporting (FAIR) approach their analysis of media bias by looking at the whole media system; they come from a tradition of media criticism. Others examine media representation of very specific issues: gay rights, freedom of speech, Religious Right, or racial identity. The distinction can make a difference, depending on how you want to build your media arsenal and approach editors or reporters with the history of media coverage of a particular issue or campaign in which you may be engaged.

Applied Research Center
3781 Broadway
Oakland, CA 94611
510-653-3415
arc@arc.org
www.arc.org
Publishes ColorLines Magazine, formerly ThirdForce, which examines coverage of ethnic minorities in media among many other issues related to social justice and community organizing.

Berkeley Media Studies Group
2140 Shattuck Ave., Ste. 804
Berkeley, CA 94704
510-204-9700
bmsg@bmsg.org
www.bmsg.org
Works with community groups and professionals to use media to advance public health policy. Monitors, studies and analyzes media to support advocacy and education.

Fairness and Accuracy in Reporting (FAIR)
112 W. 27th St.
New York, NY 10001
212-633-6700
fair@fair.org
www.fair.org
Publishes EXTRA! A bimonthly magazine of media criticism.

Gay & Lesbian Alliance Against Defamation
248 W. 35th St., 8th Fl.
New York, NY 10001
212-629-3322
glaad@glaad.org
www.glaad.org
Produces GLAADLines and GLAADAlert.

Media Alliance
942 Market St., Ste. 503
San Francisco, CA 94103
415-546-6334
info@media-alliance.org
www.media-alliance.org
Publishes MediaFile, a bimonthly journal that covers the media work environment, media ownership, and strategies for activists who want to improve news coverage.

Media Research and Action Project
Sociology Department
McGuinn Hall
Boston College
Chestnut Hill, MA 02467
617-552-8708
ryanc@bc.edu
www.bc.edu/mrap
Researches and monitors media for nonprofit organizations, as well as builds their media capacity with strategic media planning.

People for the American Way
2000 M St. NW, Ste. 400
Washington, DC 20036
800-326-7329
pfaw@pfaw.org
www.pfaw.org
Monitors and opposes efforts to suppress free expression.

Political Research Associates
1310 Broadway
Sommerville, MA 02144
617-666-5300
PublicEye@igc.apc.org
www.publiceye.org
Operates a leading clearinghouse for information on political extremists.

Rocky Mountain Media Watch
P.O. Box 18858
Denver, CA 80218
303-832-7558
newsmush@netone.com
www.bigmedia.org
Studies and analyzes local TV news to help citizens and the media understand and visualize what constitutes better journalism.

Youth Media Council
c/o Movement Strategy Center
1611 Telegraph Ave., Ste. 510
Oakland, CA 94612
510-444-0640 ext. 312
malkia@youthmediacouncil.org